Women
and the
Kingdom

FAITH & ROGER
FORSTER

Mixed Sources
Product group from well-managed
forests and other controlled sources
www.fsc.org Cert no. SGS-COC-2482
© 1996 Forest Stewardship Council
FSC

Printed and bound in Great Britain by
TJ International Ltd, Padstow, Cornwall

Contents

About the Authors

Faith and Roger Forster

In 1974 Faith and Roger Forster founded the Ichthus Christian Fellowship, which they co-lead, and currently comprises 15 London congregations, a network of 80 UK link churches and workers overseas in approximately 16 nations. Roger and Faith have three married children and four grandchildren.

Faith has been involved in Christian ministry and leadership for many years. Faith was the first woman to speak from the main platform at Spring Harvest, the first woman to serve on the executive boards of Spring Harvest, the UK Evangelical Alliance and the World Evangelical Alliance and was also the first woman on the Steering Group of the UK Charismatic Leaders' Conference. For a number of years she was a member of the Board of Moorlands Bible College. Faith believes passionately in the power of prayer and the Word of God, and loves to see lives transformed by this means.

Roger studied mathematics and theology at St John's College Cambridge. After a period in the Royal Air Force, he worked as an itinerant evangelist before starting Ichthus in 1974. Roger was one of the founders of March for Jesus, was on the board of the AD2000 Movement and the Council of the Evangelical Missionary Alliance for many years. He has been involved with the Evangelical Alliance since the early 1970s as a member of the Council, and has served on a number of EA committees. Among his many responsibilities he is Chairman of the Council for the UK Evangelical Alliance and honorary Vice President of Tearfund, and is honoured to be on the Council of Reference for Aglow International (Britain), and together with Faith is a patron of Springs Dance Company.

Roger has authored and co-authored several books, including *God's Strategy in Human History*, *Reason Science and Faith*, *Christianity Evidence and Truth*, *The Kingdom of Jesus*, *Prayer*, *Trinity* and *Suffering and the Love of God*.

Foreword

by Jackie Pullinger-To

A well known and highly respected Bible teacher asked me this question some years ago. 'Which Bible character do you most identify with?' Without pausing for thought I answered immediately 'David'. He was shocked and said he had supposed it would be a woman, like Deborah, for example. 'Why' I replied, 'would I answer in terms of gender when you asked about character?'

Since that time it has often been assumed that I feel strongly about women in Christian ministry whereas I do not. I simply believe in ministry for every believer whether old or young, male or female.

Faith and Roger have written this treatise on Women and the Kingdom which reads like a thriller. Not only did I turn the pages rapidly, it also pointed me to scripture which gave light and further understanding on what God means for individual women and their part in bringing the Kingdom of God to earth.

From time to time in the past decades the Forsters have trusted the Spirit of God in me to share with their people. They have welcomed me as a fellow worker, forgiven my weaknesses and valued the testimony of what Jesus has done in and through us in Hong Kong. Perhaps they even saw a glimpse of 'cha-yil'?

Amusingly, it has not been so with all groups. I remember the time I spoke in a famous church which had received teaching that women may not teach men. Thus I was invited to 'share your testimony' for 45 minutes whilst the male curate did the official 'teaching' for 5 minutes! A clear history of mission demonstrates that women outnumber men as missionaries and are admired and honoured for their labour on overseas fields. However, once the pagans have been won for Christ, a man must come in to lead them on! And what to do with the woman missionary when she comes back to her home country church? She has, of course, had to come under a man simply on the basis of gender rather than spiritual authority or maturity.

Long have these paradoxes existed in Christendom and I am thrilled to have scholarly and biblical exploration of the place of women in God's work. I pray this will enable both men to free women to take their place in the Kingdom, and also to let women know they have a unique individual calling. Called, not as an appendage of a man, but to a God given destiny to express Jesus.

Jackie Pullinger-To
St Stephen's Society, Hong Kong

Foreword

by Andrew Walker

It used to be thought in the early twentieth century that people who promoted women's leadership in churches – either as preachers or pastors – were liberals, and opponents of women's ministry were conservatives. Such a position in the early twenty-first century is untenable: scholarship has unearthed a treasury of women's roles in Bible and history and there is really no excuse for misreading scripture and ignoring historical evidence in the name of some supposed unmovable and immutable orthodoxy. While it is certainly the case that there are those who oppose the ministry of women in the church on principled grounds all too often the root cause is misogyny and there is no room for ambiguity here: hatred of women is sin.

Rebekah, Ruth, Miriam and Esther in the Old Testament, Dorcas and Lydia, Elizabeth, Anna, Mary Magdalene in the New Testament are women of stature not merely bit players on a stage designed to glorify men. And far too easily we forget that Jesus would never have revealed to us God's Kingdom if a certain maiden of Israel had not willingly assented to God's invitation through his messenger that she would be the mother of the Son of

God: Mary's response 'be it unto me according to thy will' was not a passive resignation but an active participation in God's love for the world.

Early Christian history is replete with women of faith equal to the Church Fathers but all too little known. The Desert Fathers are thought to have their origins in the sanctity and asceticism of St Anthony of Egypt, but it was St Mary of Egypt, the 'worker of miracles' that inspired many more to follow Christ. Or again we owe much to the Cappadocian Fathers, Basil, Gregory of Nyssa, and their friend Gregory of Nazianzus for a truly loving, personal Holy Trinity that speaks more to our generation than the functional 'modalist' model of Augustine could ever do; but none of these theologians were more intelligent, insightful and holy than Basil's sister, Macrina. And the roll call of pioneering women in the Kingdom goes on from mystics like Julian of Norwich in the Middle Ages, to Reformation heroines like the Anabaptist martyr Anneken Heyndricks and modern charismatic leaders like Kathryn Kuhlman.

To follow the biblical and historical signposts for understanding the role and significance of women in the Kingdom who can do better than a modern Aquila and Priscilla, Roger and Faith Forster. Like their New Testament counterparts they are equal partners in the Gospel. I recommend this contribution to 'right thinking' in the church by an extraordinary couple who remain loyal to their radical Christian roots but speak to us all.

Professor Andrew Walker,
CTRC, DEPS, King's College, London

Introduction

Much has been said and written on the subject of women in the Church and there has been a significant shift in women's roles, not only in the church, but in society too. For some denominations the issue has again become a seriously divisive one. As women already functioning in ministry roles are being promoted to higher offices in the Church, the underlying doctrinal differences are emerging again.

Unfortunately, even today within some church groups and denominations there is a lack of openness towards women when the question of leadership is discussed. Some church leaders appear to express sexist opinions with little or no honour shown towards the multitude of women who love God and who have poured out their lives in devoted and often costly service to him. Their potentially hurtful, if not devastating, negative remarks strike not merely at women's leadership roles, but at the nature of femininity itself, which is where the blow will be most keenly felt. Their opposition to women has far deeper implications than simply seeking to bar women from public office in Christian work, and ultimately they can rob women of their humanity and dignity.

Moreover, the sentiment put forward by some church leaders that the Church is merely following a worldly feminist agenda in opening the ranks of leadership to women, is not accurate. Historically the reverse would appear to be true. Society has been challenged and provoked by the example of Radical Church movements over the centuries. For example, the Anabaptist movement, the Quakers, John Wesley and William and Catherine Booth leading the Salvation Army, all championed the rights and equalities of women in and beyond the church despite the prevailing cultures.

This book is a plea for a reappraisal of the scriptural and historical evidence, which when correctly interpreted, in our view point to an equality of the sexes in both the life and ministry of the Church.

Our purpose is to demonstrate that our conclusions are built upon solid biblical foundations, and we aim to clearly lay out the important themes and texts, including passages, such as 1 Corinthians 11–14 and 1 Timothy 2, which have historically been used been to suppress women. Each reader, whatever their background, is encouraged to explore these for themselves and draw their own conclusions.

Please look up every reference to be fully aware of the biblical force of the arguments.

Faith and Roger Forster, London 2010

www.ichthus.org.uk

Special thanks: We would like to record our huge debt of gratitude to the women and men who have inspired us to write this book. Many women in Ichthus and in the wider Christian world have demonstrated in their lives the truths of which we have written. and some have offered valuable comments to help shape the manuscript. Particular thanks to Liz Tingman, Jenny Page and Sarah Fordham and of course to our son-in-law, Joe Laycock who has knocked the manuscript into shape!

1

Redeeming Eve

Eve's bitter legacy

> Do you not know that you are an Eve? God's verdict
> on the sex still holds good, and the sex's guilt must
> hold too. You are the Devil's gateway, you are the
> avenue to the forbidden tree. You are the first deserter
> from the law divine. It was you who persuaded him
> [Adam] whom the Devil himself had not the strength
> to assail. So lightly did you esteem God's image. For
> your deceit ... the very Son of God had to die.

With these harsh words, Tertullian, an Early Church Father (circa
160-220AD), expressed a common attitude of most Jewish and some
Christian men towards women[1]. Tertullian acquired great influence
among the Christians of his time and many commentators throughout
the generations have taken on his views without discernment. It is
no wonder that negative ideas about the female sex have polluted
the Church and God's truth ever since.

---

1 Interestingly, despite these words, in later life Tertullian joined the
Montanists, who had women leaders.

Once theological views are given influence, even if they are
contrary to what the Bible says, they are difficult to change –
especially if they become the basis of translation and interpretation,
persisting from the time of the Early Church Fathers right up to the
present day. Just because an Early Church Father said something,
does not mean that it is correct – especially when many of them
disagreed on many things.

Yet what is striking about Tertullian's words is that they are the
complete antithesis of the Bible's teaching about Eve and about
women in general. So, let us examine what the Bible does and
does not say about Eve.

God's view, as revealed from the very first chapter of the Bible,
is that women and men are both equally made in God's image. The
mandate to rule over the earth and the animals was a joint task,
equally given to both, and they were intended to work together
(Genesis 1:26-28). This proved difficult after humankind's
rebellion against God, but in the garden of Eden there was nothing
inferior about women.

It is true that it was Eve who first ate from the tree of the
knowledge of good and evil. But, as Christians we must agree that
the New Testament lays the blame for the first transgression firmly
at Adam's door. Romans 5:12-14 says that by Adam's offence
(not Eve's) sin and death entered the world. Adam was culpable
because it was he whom God had instructed not to eat from the
tree, before Eve was yet created (Genesis 2:17). Even though *she*
had eaten, God expected *him* to remain faithful to what *he* had
been commanded (Genesis 3:11,17).

It is also true that 1 Timothy 2:14 states, 'it was not Adam
who was deceived, but the woman being deceived, fell into
transgression.' However, it does not follow that from this verse
we should assume that, because Eve was deceived all women are
easily deceived, or that the female has a predisposed vulnerability

to deception. On the basis of this assumption, some consider women unfit to teach or to lead. Yet we all know women, as well as men, who have sharp, logical minds. Equally, we have all met men, as well as women, who are irrational, confused and subjective. In fact, the majority of the heresies that have invaded Christian doctrine over the centuries were invented by men, not by women! So deception cannot be seen as the sole provenance of women, as Paul himself acknowledges in 2 Corinthians 11:3. Eve was deceived because Adam did not teach her properly, just as the men and women in the Corinthian church were in danger of being deceived by false teaching in Paul's day. It was Adam's responsibility to relate God's commands to Eve correctly. Adam was not *deceived*, because he knew and understood that what he was doing was wrong – he was *disobedient*.

To her credit, Eve did not use her deception as an excuse when challenged by God (Genesis 3:13). She simply and truthfully stated what the immediate influence was that led her to eat the fruit. It was Satan and his snare that induced her to fall and she accused the serpent openly to God. By exposing Satan's activity in this way she provoked hostility against herself – as God emphasized when he said to Satan, 'I will put enmity between you and the woman' (Genesis 3:15). Far from implying that woman was in league with Satan, as Tertullian's quote suggests, and therefore would be so for evermore, the Bible reveals Eve as Satan's antagonist. Eve created a breach between herself and the Enemy by her exposure of Satan, and God widened it. God promised that she would ultimately cause Satan's downfall through Jesus, her 'seed'.

It is interesting to compare this with Gideon in Judges 6: God commanded him to tear down the altar of Baal and he eventually obeyed, under cover of night. When his deeds were exposed, he was named 'Jerubbaal', which means 'Let Baal contend against him', or 'Baal's enemy'. In a similar way woman became Satan's enemy. His animosity towards her has been demonstrated throughout the ages and around the world, as women have been despised, oppressed and treated cruelly.

It is interesting to note that although Satan also indirectly caused Adam's disobedience by working on him through Eve, Adam does not acknowledge Satan's part in the affair. When God asks him, 'Have you eaten from the tree?' he replies, 'The woman whom *you* gave to be with me, *she* gave me of the tree and I ate ...' (italics ours). Adam acknowledges Eve's part, but puts the blame on God instead of Satan as the indirect cause. Satan, who appears to have been present at the interview, or at least nearby (v14), must have rejoiced to see Adam add to his disobedience the sin of charging God with some responsibility for it. Surely these bad character traits – deliberate, conscious disobedience and evasion of responsibility – should disqualify Adam from leading others, just as much as deception might disqualify Eve. Yet we do not tend to assume that all men are automatically unfit to lead or to teach on this basis.

In fact, while the Bible does not disparage Eve's character at all, it does have some rather strong words to say about Adam. For example, Job says, 'Have I covered my transgressions like Adam, by hiding my iniquity in my bosom?' (Job 31:33), and Hosea says, 'Like Adam they have transgressed the covenant, there they have dealt treacherously against me' (Hosea 6:7).

In the New Testament the language becomes even stronger: 'through one man sin entered into the world ... death reigned from Adam until Moses ... By the transgression of the one, the many died ... By the transgression of the one, death reigned through the one ... through the one man's disobedience the many were made sinners ...' (Romans 5:12-19).

It has been suggested that Adam was theologically the first to sin, because he put himself in a feminine role by following his wife in blatant disobedience, that is, he sinned because he should govern his wife, not the other way round. This idea is unwarranted by the context – Adam knew not to eat from the tree, but Eve did not[2]. Strictly, the Bible does not say that Adam was 'the first to sin', but rather, that '*through his sin death entered into the world*' (italics ours). By comparison, in the story of Ananias and Sapphira (Acts 5:1-11) we see that Sapphira was judged for an act of blatant disobedience: '…why is it that you have agreed together...?' Peter did not suggest that Sapphira was simply being 'feminine' by following Ananias, but that by being complicit in his deception she was equally culpable, and they both suffered the same fate.

Chrysostom, an Early Church Father, points out that in Romans 5 Paul is saying that 'it was not the actual sin of the transgression of the law, but that of the *disobedience of Adam* – this was what brought universal destruction' (italics ours).

Apocryphal influences

In the light of the New Testament interpretation of the Fall and Adam's guilt, it seems even stranger that men such as Tertullian should make so much of Eve's guilt. Where did he get his ideas from, since they plainly do not come from Holy Scripture? Undoubtedly, he was influenced by some Jewish writings called *Ecclesiasticus*, or *The Wisdom of Ben Sira*, written around 250BC and widely circulated among Jews. These writings, set down at a time when Judaism was apostate, unspiritual and heavily influenced by the pagan cultures that surrounded it, were the source of much of the Talmudic teaching concerning the Fall[3]. *The Wisdom of Ben Sira* states baldly: 'From women a beginning of sin: and because of her all die.' We may safely say that the Talmud does not represent Christian, or even Biblical teaching!

The Talmud includes over forty citations from Ben Sira, from where it largely draws its teaching about the Fall. The account of

---

2 If the roles had been reversed and Eve had wilfully sinned because her husband had incited her then the judgements would surely have been reversed also.

3 The Talmud is the Jewish collection of case law – 'The tradition of the elders', criticized by Jesus in Mark 7:8-9 – passed down orally and collected together with the rabbinic commentaries on this material.

Eve's deception seems to have been overlaid by the pagan myth
of Pandora, who opened a box of evil, represented by creatures,
which escaped into the world. The Talmud, enlarging on Eve's
guilt, lists ten 'curses' which were supposedly uttered against
Eve. They include the 'traditional' views that woman is cursed
in childbearing and childrearing; in inordinate sexual desire for
her husband; in his ruling over her; and in her duty to dress like
a mourner and not appear in public with uncovered head. Thus
far, some Christians might agree with the Talmud. However, few
would approve the two remaining 'curses' listed:

   i) That a woman is restricted to one husband while he
      may have many wives, and

   ii) That she should be confined to the house as to a prison!

But did God really curse Eve? It seems to say so in our modern
translations. However, Hebrew scholar Katherine Bushnell[4] has
questioned this translation by looking at the original texts. She
maintains that by revocalization and drawing on the Septuagint
reading, the phrase 'I will greatly multiply your pain in childbearing'
(Genesis 3:16) could equally well be translated: 'A snare has
increased your sorrow and your sighing'[5]. This would be an obvious
reference to Satan's lying in wait to deceive Eve and the resulting
oppression from Satan and from man who would 'rule over her'.

Even if some do not go with Bushnell's perceptive rendering of
the text, it is still evident that Eve would indeed have sorrow, as
would the man, since he would now find nature itself opposing him

---

4   See Katherine C. Bushnell, *God's Word to Women* (available free online at
    www.godswordtowomen.org)

5   The inspired Hebrew texts were written with no vowels or punctuation.
    When copying them, the Masorites inserted vowels. Textual rendering, i.e.
    which vowels to insert, is usually obvious from the words and their context,
    however problems arise when more than one possible reading exists.
    Revocalisation is when alternative vowels are inserted into the original
    consonants. It is here that theological bias could lead to one reading being
    inserted rather than another, equally valid one.

in his labour to grow food, especially once he is expelled from the Garden. The bringing forth of human life and sustaining it will be a struggle. Here, God is describing what will happen as a consequence of their sin, not determining it – he is explaining, not cursing.

Does an understanding of these Genesis verses really matter? Yes, because the teachings of the Apocrypha and the Talmud have found their way into 'Christian' teaching and have greatly influenced the interpretation and translation of verses relating to women. Some Early Church Fathers quoted from these writings as if they were authoritative, and this is undoubtedly why Eve has had such a bad press ever since. As the first representative of the female sex, that is unwelcome news for all women.

What God says about Eve

Yet God makes the most wonderful statements both to and about Eve. Let's look again at what God says. First, in the words addressed to Satan, God says: 'I will put enmity between you and the woman, and between your seed and her seed. He shall bruise you on the head and you shall bruise him on the heel' (Genesis 3:15).

We have already thought about the enmity between Satan and the woman, but what about the enmity between his seed and her seed? Who are Eve's 'seed'? In the next sentence it is clear that God is alluding ultimately to Jesus, the coming Deliverer who would bruise the serpent's head. But the 'seed' may be taken to mean not just one person but many. Some have thought it means the whole human race, but this is precluded by the statement that Satan's seed would oppose Eve's. 'Satan's children' usually designates morally and spiritually corrupt human beings [6]. Whom, therefore, do those evil people oppose? None other than Eve's seed. Paul writes to believers in Romans 16:20 – 'The God of peace shall bruise Satan under your feet shortly' (KJV).

The inference is that *believers* are Eve's seed. Those who trust

6   See Matthew 13:38; John 6:70; John 8:42-44; 1 John 3:7-10

the promise of God and maintain the conflict with Satan are Eve's children. She showed herself a believer in the promise of God concerning the coming Redeemer who would bruise Satan's head [7]. For God promised that through her would come the Deliverer. Perhaps this is why, when Adam was confronted with the sentence of death which he had brought on himself and on the whole human race, he called his wife 'Eve' – literally 'life spring' – and the Bible adds that this was because she was 'the mother of all living'. Since this follows God's promise concerning her seed, it is quite possible that 'all living' refers only to believers too. In other words, Adam recognised his wife as a spring of spiritual life whose seed would overcome the death that he had brought into the world. Charles Wesley captured the spirit of this in two lines of his famous carol *Hark the Herald Angels Sing* when he wrote:

> Rise, thou woman's conquering seed,
> Bruise in us the serpent's head!

Finally, in Genesis 3:22-24 it was the man, not the woman whom God specifically expelled from the Garden of Eden. Eve is not named in the 'sending out', but it is evident from the context that she follows her husband. Thus she too, like Adam, loses the place of total security and immortality. From now on her fruitfulness and authority (Genesis 1:27) will be challenged and warred against by Satan until the time of the Messiah's final victory. When Mary offers herself to God as a channel for divine life (Luke 1:38), she becomes in her own person the one to fulfil the promise to Eve that the seed of the woman shall bruise the serpent's head. The angel's greeting to Mary as he brings her the good news ought to be engraved on the heart and spirit of every woman who loves God and offers herself to him as his 'servant' and life-bearer: 'Hail, favoured one! The Lord is with you…'

---

7   Cf. her cry of joy, albeit misplaced, when she gave birth to Cain, in Genesis 4:1
   – 'I have gotten a man, the LORD', NASB margin.

2

Old Testament Oppression?

In the beginning it was not so

It is often said that in the Old Testament Israel was a patriarchal society – a man's world – and that if that was the case, then maybe God wanted it that way. But does the Old Testament consistently give a subordinate place to women, or was society less hierarchical and more respectful of women than is popularly assumed today?

Right from the beginning of the Bible there is a strong suggestion, not of matriarchy (women in power), but certainly of a bias towards a *matrilocal* practice (residence with the wife's family) in God's first directive concerning marriage in Genesis 2:24 – 'For this reason a man shall leave his father and his mother and be joined to his wife, and they shall become one flesh.' Anthropologists have discovered widespread evidence of the practice of a man leaving his home on marriage and joining his wife in her family home or location in the ancient world. If this is true, it would have ensured that the wife was properly respected and her interests protected by her family if necessary. It would have been much more difficult for a man to enslave his wife in this scenario, than has been the case throughout much of later history, where a woman would leave her household to become the new and vulnerable member of her husband's.

When, in turn, God called Abraham, Isaac and Jacob to found a new nation, it was not automatically assumed that the wives they married would go with them on their wanderings, as we shall see in this chapter. Following on from Eve, a picture of the Old Testament begins to emerge which, while not matriarchal, is seemingly less patriarchal than is often assumed. Let's take a look at some of the women in the Old Testament and see what we can understand about the ways in which women were viewed and treated.

Sarah

God honoured and exalted Sarah alongside Abraham, by changing both of their names: Abram, 'exalted father', became Abraham, 'father of a multitude', and 'as for Sarai ... Sarah shall be her name' (Genesis 17:15). The name Sarah means 'chieftainess' or 'female ruler', from the ancient Eastern term *sar* which means 'chief'. Our modern Bibles usually render the translation as 'princess', but this is unfortunate, as to us the word generally denotes the wife of a prince or the daughter of a king, rather than a ruler in her own right. Yet this name was given to Sarah in order to affirm her authority as chieftainess of the new nation God was founding. 'Sarai' means 'my princess' and 'Sarah' means 'the princess'. The first restricts the function of her name to Abraham, but the second generalizes it to all mankind – it was not given in order for Abraham to assert his authority over her, but to *strengthen her own authority*.

Some have thought that the modern practice of a wife taking her husband's surname after marriage is a legacy of Adam's action in naming his wife Eve, and expresses his authority over her. In reality this practice dates back only a few centuries in the Western world. It was instituted in order to strengthen the family bonds by giving the father the acknowledged right to 'own' his children, and to make public record keeping easier. There is no evidence that men 'named' their wives at all in the Bible, except in the special case of Eve, which we looked at earlier and that shows no hint of interest in Adam's authority over her.

We see God honouring Sarah again when he describes her as one of his 'anointed ones' in 1 Chronicles 16:22 and in Psalm 105:15. When the two Abimelechs[1] were told 'not to touch' God's anointed, it was specifically *Sarah* who was named in the first instance (Genesis 20:6) and both Isaac and Rebekah in the second (Genesis 26:11). Sarah was undoubtedly God's anointed or chosen one, for despite the low value Abraham apparently put on her, by allowing her to be taken into a pagan king's harem with little human hope of her emerging untouched, if at all, God nonetheless protected and rescued her, and it was she who eventually received power to conceive the promised child by faith (Hebrews 11:11). Because God valued Sarah more than Abraham did, Isaac was eventually born as the first in line to the promised 'anointed one'.

In fact, God later directed Abraham to obey *Sarah* in whatever *she* said to him (Genesis 21:12), using the same word 'obey' here as in Genesis 22:18 when God praises Abraham's obedience to his own voice. This needs to be borne in mind when reading Peter's encouragement to Christian wives to have a respectful and submissive attitude to their husbands, using Sarah as an example (1 Peter 3:1-7).

The only occasion where Sarah humourously refers to Abraham as her 'lord' was in regard to them having intercourse together in order to conceive the promised child. In other words it expressed her sexual submission to her husband even though she was 90 years old (cf. 1 Corinthians 7:4)! Perhaps this was in Peter's mind, since he refers to husband and wife in the next verse as 'fellow heirs of the grace of life', as they bring forth children together.

---

1 Abimelech means 'father-king' and is a title, not a proper name

Rebekah

Later on in Genesis, Abraham's servant, when commissioned to seek a bride for Isaac from among Abraham's relatives (Genesis 24:5), seems to assume that she might well insist on Isaac's going to live with her family, and not the other way round.

Moreover, when the servant arrives and asks for Bethuel (Rebekah's father) Rebekah runs to 'her *mother's* house' (Genesis 24:28, italics ours), from where an invitation to stay is issued to the servant, and both her mother and father are involved in the transaction. However, Rebekah had already issued an invitation (v24), indicating that she had the right to do so. These references seem to underscore the assertion that women in those days had rights of property over the matrimonial home. The story is further illuminating as to the dignity and independence of women, in that Rebekah was given the free choice: to go with the servant and marry Isaac, or not (Genesis 24:58). It was to her *mother* (not her father), and to Rebekah's brother that the servant gave gifts, after chiefly bestowing them on Rebekah herself. In fact, it is *Isaac* rather than Rebekah who does not seem to be consulted in this 'arranged marriage'.

We see a similar picture when we look at Genesis 31. In verse 38 we see that Jacob had joined himself to his wives' family for twenty years. In verses 4-16 it is evident that Jacob is giving his wives the *choice* of going with him back to his native land or staying with their father – he is treating them as equals. They choose to leave the pagan, scheming Laban in order to go with Jacob on his pilgrimage with God. This is in part because Laban had cheated them out of their rights and their inheritance – literally 'our money' in verse 15.

Perhaps these examples will serve to demonstrate that women had rights and status in the ancient world and were not mere chattels. To some extent at least, the patriarchs clearly respected the women they married as independent agents, and certainly deemed them worthy of honour.

Miriam

Several women are named as prophets in the Old Testament, who exercised leadership authority as well as received messages from God. First is Miriam, whom God himself describes as a leader in Micah 6:4, alongside Aaron and Moses. It is interesting to see that when she criticized Moses, who was 'more meek than any man on the face of the earth', God took Miriam's arrogance very seriously (and Aaron's, but she appears to have been more culpable) and judged her severely for it (Numbers 12). Moses graciously interceded for her and she was healed after seven days, but the people of God could not move on until she was restored to them.

The point is that 'to whom much is given, much is required', and this is true for both men and women. God's action in disciplining Miriam without altogether rejecting her is evidence of his affirmation of her (see Hebrews 12:6).

Deborah

Deborah was not merely a prophet but a judge. The Hebrew verb 'to judge' – *shaphat* – used to describe Deborah in Judges 4:4 is the same word used some twenty times in the book of Judges, and also of Samuel and the kings (1 Samuel 7–8), for those who delivered Israel from their enemies (Judges 2:16).

To any unbiased reader, Judges chapters 4 and 5 leave little doubt that Deborah was the leader of God's people at that time. Quite apart from the fact that 'the sons of Israel' came to her magisterial seat under the palm tree between Ramah and Bethel in order to have their disputes settled, there is no mistaking the authoritative tone in Deborah's words and actions. We are told that she 'sent and summoned Barak' in order to deliver the word of God's command to him. Barak's insistence on Deborah's accompanying him into the battle against Sisera and his army was surely a need to be assured of God's presence, epitomized by the person of his representative, Deborah, in this apparently crazy venture, not a wimpish intention to hide behind a woman's skirt! At any rate, Deborah readily agreed as she had no doubt about the outcome of the battle, having received it by divine revelation.

She had also been informed by God that the ultimate glory, that of slaying Sisera himself, would go to a woman, for it was Jael who drove the tent peg through Sisera's head as he slept, in the final dramatic touch of this story. This is not exactly a prettily feminine action, but when one considers the character of Sisera and his history of capturing, robbing and ravishing women (Judges 5:30), it is entirely fitting that the wrath and aggression of these two women, Deborah and Jael, should be aroused against him.

Deborah celebrates this victory of two women over a captor and despoiler of women in a striking and beautiful song (Judges 5), the opening line of which has caused some headaches to translators. Here are some of the renderings:

> That the leaders took the lead in Israel … (RSV)

> For the avenging of Israel … (AV)

> In the breaking forth of the breakers … (Cambridge)

> That the strong in Israel showed themselves strong …
> (Keil and Delitzsh)

> That the leaders led in Israel … (NASB)

The important point is that the subject of this sentence is a *feminine* form, being the plural participle of the same verb as the predicate, i.e. leaders leading. This verb is *para*, which means 'to loose, let go', and the verbal noun is in the feminine form, not the masculine, which would have been used if it were referring to male leaders. Thus to read it emphatically as 'leaders', i.e. ruling men, is unwarranted. A more literal rendering of the phrase would be:

> That the loosing (free-ifying) female ones loosed
> (freed) Israel … Bless the Lord!

This sits well with the context of this story, the freeing of Israel from an ugly oppressor by two women. Deborah continues: 'The peasantry ceased, they ceased in Israel, until I, Deborah, arose, until I arose, a mother in Israel.' Deborah was not merely maternal, but matriarchal in her role in this story, and she reveals the source of her authority and strength, and that of all godly women, in the beautiful ending to her song: 'Let those who love him be like the rising of the sun in its might.'

Huldah

Huldah is the third woman prophet we will discuss here, leaving aside Isaiah's wife, who is also called a prophet (Isaiah 8:3). Huldah came to national prominence in the reign of Josiah (2 Chronicles 34). When the king sent Hilkiah the priest to enquire of Huldah concerning the condition of himself and the people in the light of the book of law, which they had just rediscovered, her answer to the king 'does not betray anything of that trembling diffidence and abject servility which some people think should characterize the ministry of women.'[2] Huldah's prophetic word was delivered with authority and dignity, and the king received it as the word of the Lord.

The strong woman ... more precious than rubies

With regard to 'strong women', we should point out that the ancient world did not have the same distaste towards women of character that some men now seem to have. In Ruth 3:11 Boaz says to Ruth 'All my people in the city know that you are a woman of *cha-yil*.' King Lemuel (Proverbs 31:10) says: 'A woman of *cha-yil* who can find? Her worth is far above jewels.'

What does this Hebrew word *cha-yil* actually mean? It is used 242 times in the Old Testament, in over 200 of which it is translated as 'army', 'war', 'host', 'forces', 'might', 'power',

---

2 *Female Ministry*, Catherine Booth, 1870

'soldiers', strength', 'valour', 'violently' or 'strong'. The remaining occurrences of *cha-yil* are either translated as 'able', 'worthy' or 'wealthy', with the exception of twice when it is used in connection with women, where modern translations prefer to use 'excellent', 'virtuous' or 'noble'.

This does not bring out the force of the word originally used, possibly because translators have thought it a less popular adjective with which to describe a woman today – maybe because some men fear that a strong woman will be a threat to them, being somehow less biddable. Some of the old translations however, rendered *cha-yil* in its usual sense of 'strong' or 'powerful'.

The Septuagint[3] translates Proverbs 31:10 as:

> 'A masculine woman who can find?'

and the Syriac text[4] makes her qualities even plainer:

> 'A strong, powerful, virile woman who can find?'

God's ancient people seemed to admire a strong woman. This is hardly surprising since it is women of weak undisciplined character who are more likely to be led astray, morally and doctrinally (2 Timothy 3:6). We should take our stand with the apostle Paul when he urges: 'Let a woman *learn* ...' (italics ours). Strength of mind and an honourable character (Proverbs 31:25) come from knowing and loving God and his word (v26).

Some people are afraid of strong women and think that to be ruled by women is a symptom of moral and spiritual decadence, which they infer from their reading of Isaiah 3:12;

> Children oppress my people and women rule over them.

---

3 The Septuagint is the oldest translation of the Hebrew Bible into Greek dating from between the third and first centuries BC

4 The Syriac Peshitta is the oldest translation of the Hebrew Bible into Aramaic, circa first century AD

However, most commentators have long recognized that this translation is very debatable. While an in-depth study of the possible translations is beyond the scope of this book, here we simply point out that the Septuagint translates this verse:

> As for my people, tax-gatherers glean them and
> exacters [extortioners] rule over them.

This is not only an equally acceptable rendering of the Hebrew, but also more consistent with the sense of the following verses, particularly verse 14, when the 'princes' with whom God takes issue are masculine in the Hebrew, not feminine. This is consistent with the context of Assyrian oppression which Isaiah is prophesying about.

Jezebel – The Dreaded Exception

We cannot conclude this chapter without taking a quick look at Jezebel – the Old Testament character any woman would be horrified at being likened to (and the character most likely to 'spook' male leaders). In the Christian world, Jezebel is sometimes held up by men as a figure of warning, of what a strong woman could become, or even what femininity is in its essence. The concept which has been suggested, of a 'Jezebel spirit' that enters women and drives them to dominate men, is enough to reduce many good people to quivering wrecks! We wish to challenge this fear-fuelled notion.

However, since we believe totally in the spiritual world and in the existence of evil spirits, we acknowledge that it is possible to have a spirit seek to enter the lives of men and women in pastoral leadership, so that the effect of their ministry is oppressive and spiritually contaminated, instead of liberating. In Spirit-filled churches where spirituality is prized, this is plainly a route that Satan might seek to use to infiltrate the Church. Therefore, it is worth us looking at the Jezebel spirit from a biblical perspective.

In the New Testament we see a woman called Jezebel working

havoc in the Early Church (Revelation 2:20-23). The words of warning about this woman have some correlation with the picture of Jezebel in the Old Testament, so it is probably worth us taking a look at her and her sins.

Who is Jezebel?

The woman Jezebel is described in 1 Kings 16–21, and 2 Kings 9:30-37. She was a pagan princess whom king Ahab of Israel married. She is described as inciting her (already evil) husband, Ahab, to even greater wickedness (1 Kings 16:30-33; 1 Kings 21:25). Jezebel was an arrogant woman, who brought into Israel occultic Baal and Asherah worship, whose practices were immoral and degenerate. She hated the prophets of Jehovah, particularly Elijah, because she was driven by the spirits of her own religion.

She was also unscrupulous in her moral behaviour, appropriating Naboth's vineyard for her husband despite the fact that it was Naboth's family inheritance. Her unrestrained arrogance moved her to use religious means (proclaiming a fast) to add power to her false accusations against Naboth, resulting in his death. There was 'no fear of God before her eyes'. However, it is obvious that Ahab sanctioned her evil behaviour and was a participant in it. He was the lawful king of Israel but did not seek to impose the values of Israel on his wife's behaviour. Ahab abdicated all his responsibility to spiritually guide the nation of Israel, which God had entrusted to him (not to Jezebel). What can we conclude of the sins of Jezebel? She was:

    a) moved by an occultic spirit
    b) engaged in false spirituality
    c) was a thief, a liar and a murderer
    d) hated the true prophets
    e) despised family loyalties and inheritance
    f) used her position and power to threaten and intimidate.

While it is not impossible that such a woman could find her way into today's churches, she is surely unlikely to be in leadership of a godly fellowship! We would be quite wrong in attributing a 'Jezebel spirit' to someone who simply has a strong personality. Similarly, it is wrong to attribute it to someone who is merely bossy, domineering or manipulative (which are not acceptable traits in Christian leadership and need to be corrected in both men and women). But a 'Jezebel-like spirit' is distinct and will have deeper spiritual effects on families and on true prophetic prayers. It comes from a sexually licentious and occult source, which originates in a rebellious world.[5]

We do not say that we will never find this kind of spirit operating in the Church, because false spirituality and a form of occult mysticism can sometimes be found as a counterfeit wherever the Holy Spirit has begun to work. We need to be alert for ungodly, unsubmissive 'spirituality', wherever it manifests. We merely plead that we do not slander women who aspire to true godliness and good order by attaching such a horrible label to them. It would be a very damning thing for any Christian woman to be described as 'a Jezebel', let alone a woman who is seeking to serve the Lord by pastoring the flock of God. If women (in leadership or otherwise) are manifesting the negative aspects of femininity, other leaders should surely follow Paul's direction: 'If anyone is caught in any trespass, you who are spiritual, restore such a one in a spirit of gentleness; each one looking to yourself, so that you too will not be tempted' (Galatians 6:1). Presumably they were appointed originally because of their spiritual strengths, so we should appeal to those if necessary.

In the New Testament, we see this woman called Jezebel in Revelation 2:20-23. She is described as a self-appointed, false-teaching prophet. The fruit of her 'ministry' was immorality and

---

5 See Francis Frangipane, *The Three Battlegrounds* (Advancing Church, 1989)

involvement with idols and false worship, which damaged the church. Because of her arrogant and unrepentant attitude and practices God states that he will judge her severely.

In addition to these two named 'Jezebels', we see the character and spirit of Jezebel working through Herodias (Mark 6:17-28). She hated and persecuted God's prophet, John the Baptist (the new Elijah) just as Jezebel had hated Elijah of old. In fact her murderous hatred did not stop until she had manipulated her husband into having John put to death and having his head served up on a platter at their licentious feast. It would be hard to find an example which more clearly exhibited the spirit of Jezebel at work than this.

Then we see the ultimate depiction of Jezebel in the harlot of Babylon described in Revelation 17–18. In her vanity, arrogance immorality, idolatry and implacable hatred towards God's servants, she is the personification of all the evil Jezebel spirits of history and she rides on the Beast, who represents the male-type sins of murder, threats, violence and blasphemy. There are many correlations in the descriptions of the harlot in Revelation and Jezebel in the Old Testament. In fact, the harlot is the embodiment of the worst sins of woman, showing how evil will manifest itself in the last days.

Over the years, we have sadly encountered some male and some female leaders who have behaved in controlling, manipulative, and even deceitful ways. We have also occasionally known of female and male leaders who have drawn from spiritual streams which do not bear good fruit, but cause damage to families and to the spiritual life of the church. Such people should be avoided and prayed for, resisted and if necessary condemned, but always in a spirit of grace. Very often they have themselves been led astray by others, or by their own brokenness, and need help from those around them.

The great strength of men and women working together and respecting each other, is that we can help one another to grow in grace and godliness. Together we can show the world why God made us 'male and female' and gave us leadership together (Genesis 1:28). This is a solemn charge from the Lord to men and women and, properly exercised, will guard us from the inroads of Jezebelic spirits into the Church.

Conclusion

In concluding this chapter we re-iterate that we do not disagree with the traditional view that the general trend of society in the Old Testament was patriarchal, but we are concerned to show the real honour given to godly women in the ancient world. Often their gifts and authority were accepted not just by individuals, but by the whole of society. Furthermore, we have clearly demonstrated that God does not show a disapproval of women in leadership.

The Old Testament was accepted by Jesus as authoritative, and even though he deepened and reinterpreted it, he never rejected it (John 10:35). Instead, he followed its example of giving honour, value and praise to women.

3

The New Humanity

The Overlap of the Ages

As Christians we are living in the overlap between two ages (1 Corinthians 10:11). The Kingdom has come (Romans 14:17), yet it has not (2 Timothy 4:1). We reign in life by one man, Christ Jesus (Romans 5:17), but wait for a future heavenly Kingdom (1 Corinthians 4:8). Believers taste the power of the age to come (Hebrew 6:5), before the presence of that age is established. We have resurrection now (Philippians 3:10), but must not say that resurrection is past (2 Timothy 2:18). Already we have come to the heavenly Jerusalem (Hebrews 12:22), which one day will come down to us (Revelation 21:10).

Since we are in this overlap of the ages, we anticipate the future here and now. We have already put on a humanity which belongs to an age to come. In this new humanity, as we shall see, there is no room for discrimination on the basis of nationality, class or sex.

So, living in the Church age we are influenced by both the past age and the age to come. As a result, we are caught in a tension of conflicts between, on one hand, our created and natural distinctions, and on the other, the supernatural ideals which shall be for ever, and towards which we want to strive. We long for greater expression of this new humanity where familiar creatorial distinctions are subsumed into a truly egalitarian community of love and justice.

The new humanity in the New Testament

All New Testament teaching may be found either as explicit or embryonic in the teaching and example of the Lord Jesus. The new vision of society, afterwards to be developed in the Epistles and Revelation, is anticipated in Mark 12:18-27.

> Is this not the reason you are mistaken, that you do not understand the Scriptures or the power of God? For when they rise from the dead, they neither marry nor are given in marriage, but are like angels in heaven.
>
> Mark 12:24-25

Here Jesus refers to the coming age of resurrection life and is aware of the tensions and problems it evokes in the Sadducees as the future breaks into the present Church Age[1]. Just as national and class distinctions will be irrelevant at the resurrection, so too, Jesus affirms, will the distinction between the sexes.

It is the Holy Spirit who leads us into all truth (John 16:13), including the truth of the Scriptures. If we are to avoid the Lord's judgement in Mark 12, we too must know the Scriptures and their teaching, but only in and by the power of God who enables us to participate in their truth and the destiny they set before us.

Paul affirms that this new humanity, freed from eathly distinctions, applies to the redeemed society of the Church.

> For all of you who were baptized into Christ have clothed yourselves with Christ. There is neither Jew nor

---

1 When does the Church Age actually begin? Was it at the resurrection, ascension, or at Pentecost? In Luke 16:16 Jesus states 'The Law and the Prophets were proclaimed until John; since that time the gospel of the Kingdom of God has been preached', so the Church Age seemingly begins at Jesus' baptism.

> Greek, there is neither slave nor free, there is not male
> and female [NASB margin, alluding to Genesis 1:27],
> for you are all one in Christ Jesus.　　Galatians 3:27-8

This is in stark contrast to a passage in the Talmud that states, 'A Jewish man is obligated to say the following prayer every day: Thank you God for not making me a Gentile, a woman or a slave.' Other examples of rabbinic teaching include, 'Let the words of the Law be burned rather than committed to a woman', 'If a man teaches his daughter the Law it is as though he teaches her lechery' and 'He who talks with a woman in public brings evil upon himself'. These and other such teachings became enshrined in Jewish law, and it was into this culture that Jesus and Paul were born, which serves to highlight just how counter-cultural both of them were.

If we are being raised up and seated in 'heavenly places in Christ Jesus' (Ephesians 2:6), where no discrimination of authority or value is made on the basis of race, social status or gender, then surely we should try to emulate Paul and Jesus as far as possible on earth.

Setting the captives free

Sexism, racism, slavery and poverty are seen throughout the Old Testament, but they are routinely and consistently shown to be contrary to God's intention for mankind. In the New Testament, Jesus' gospel proclamation of Isaiah 61 (Luke 4:18) struck these oppressive structures at root, by changing the hearts of the oppressors and lifting up the oppressed. That there should be a class of people condemned to perpetual poverty; that there should be people who have no choice but to be slaves; that there should be whole races locked into inferiority of status; and that half of humankind should be made subservient to the other half on the grounds of sex – all these inequalities have been dealt a death blow by the gospel, which shows the way of redemption, freedom and blessing for all classes and conditions of men and women.

Of course, not everyone agrees with these sentiments. For example, at the time of William Wilberforce many slave owners argued fiercely that slavery was an institution that God upheld, and they 'proved' it not just from Old Testament Scriptures, but from the fact that, although Jesus proclaimed freedom for captives, he made no statement directly demanding the freeing of slaves. Nor did he liberate any slave by choosing one to be among the twelve apostles. Precisely the same kind of statement could be made by Judaizers about the Jew-Gentile question. Jesus rarely preached to Gentiles, and no Gentile was called to be one of the twelve. We could even argue, on that basis, that Jesus upheld the superiority of Jews (Mark 7:27). Nevertheless, we do not find that the Early Church continually kept Gentiles or slaves out of leadership, despite the advantages that Jews had in being already familiar with the Scriptures. When Peter was tempted to treat Gentiles as spiritually inferior, he was rebuked twice, first by God (Acts 10:15,28) and then by Paul (Galatians 2:11-16).

Concerning the issue of slavery in the early nineteenth century, many committed Christians, such as Charles Finney who campaigned to abolish slavery, recognized that the arguments for the emancipation of women were essentially the same. Those who favoured the practice of slavery used many of the same points as those who argued for the subjection of women to men:

i   the absence of any statement by Jesus clearly speaking against such subjection

ii   teaching of the apostles that seems positively to uphold the master-slave relationship

iii the apparent acceptance of the prevailing social order by Jews and the fact that no slave was numbered among the apostles

iv   the desirability of maintaining the current social order to avoid uncomfortable disturbance.

The abolitionists for their part pointed out that, while it is true that Jesus did little to trim the branches of the unacceptable tree by speaking out directly against it, he did something far more radical. In his actions and his teachings about human relationships he dealt a blow to the root of that tree, which would ensure the withering and toppling of the whole structure if his words were received and heeded. The pastoral directives written by the apostles could be seen as the restraining 'ropes' around the 'tree' as it is being felled – restraints to prevent the tree from falling in an uncontrolled way and causing damage. Again, parallels can be seen here with regard to how the apostles dealt with the issue of women.

God's new people

The power of God and the Scriptures both lead us to express our new humanity now. This means that sex discrimination in church life, as well as discrimination on the basis of class or race, is to be prayerfully and carefully guarded against. However, we will be aware of the tensions caused by being clothed in our earthly bodies of humiliation (Philippians 3:21) that belong to the age of creation, while earnestly longing to be clothed with our bodies of the age of redemption (2 Corinthians 5:2).

Clearly the Lord Jesus was aware of such difficulties among men and women. We were created for monogamous and faithful marriage (Matthew 19:3-9). Jesus' disciples were appalled at such high expected standards and responded with: 'If the relationship of the man with his wife is like this, it is better not to marry.' Evidently the demands of marriage and its inviolability, as given by God in Genesis 2 and reaffirmed by Jesus in Matthew 19, were felt by the disciples to be an impossible goal. In our condition as fallen creatures faithful and monogomous marriage is a rare achievement.

But at this point a new people, the Church, is coming into being, consisting of two groups of Christians: married and unmarried. The married are seeking to restore their created role as given before man's fall, in God-gifted oneness. They are aware that they belong to the old created order, though they are moving on as 'fellow heirs', as Peter would say, heirs of the future hope of Christlikeness in resurrection (1 Peter 1:3-4; 3:7).

The second group of Christians are the unmarried. Some of these may inherit their unmarried condition from the way they were made, for others it may be the result of their environment. Still others may, like Christ, and later Paul, anticipate the sexless age by choosing celibacy 'for the sake of the Kingdom' (Matthew 19:12).

Both types of Christians make up the Church at present. Both are equally honourable and both reflect the condition of the age to come: the one, the love of Christ for his bride, and the other, the angelic condition of our coming service for him. Both require different aspects of the grace, which God distributed to all men (e.g. Matthew 19:11; 1 Corinthians 7:7). Both are legitimate callings from God that we recognize and take seriously as we wait for the 'age to come'.

Paul's 'restrictions'?

Jesus' teaching is the foundation on which Paul expresses and builds this truth of the new humanity – 'no male and female' – in Christ. Surely then, it should be unthinkable that discrimination should exist at all in the great adventure to perfect humanity and true society in the Church.

However, there are three passages, and only three (or really two since 1 Corinthians 11–14 is a single section on church order), in which the apostle Paul appears in some way to place restrictions upon women: 1 Corinthians 11:1-16, 1 Corinthians 14:34-40 and 1 Timothy 2:9-15.

Yet, as we will see in chapters 6–9, it may be that these are not restrictions, but evidence of the tensions of the overlap of the ages – restraining ropes around the falling trees of racial, sexual and economic discrimination – and require guidance and insight as to their interpretation. Before looking at these passages in detail, let us consider more fully the example of our Lord Jesus and how he treated women.

4

Unique Jesus

Jesus' attitude towards women

When we look at the person of Jesus as he is revealed in the Gospels, we encounter that amazing radiance which emanates from his unique personhood. Only the very hardened, or the incurably religious, can fail to be moved by the man Jesus. If, as Paul declared and we believe, he is the express image of the invisible God (Colossians 1:15) – what a God we have! His authority is demonstrated with such a light touch, his humility is firm and unable to be manipulated, and over all there is the compelling power of vibrant life. As those whose primary calling is to proclaim Jesus, we are overwhelmingly grateful to have such good news to share!

Jesus is particularly good news for women. This is powerfully true today, but how much more so in the first century AD. We have seen how women were viewed at that time as second class citizens, little better than slaves.

When Jesus first revealed his 'mission statement' in Luke 4:18-19 – to preach the gospel to the poor, proclaim release to the captives, recovery of sight to the blind and freedom to those

who were oppressed – he unveiled God's great liberating power
for all humanity. The proclamation of the favourable year of the
Lord encompassed the poor, the sick, slaves, Gentiles and women
– these were the people who Jesus came to release. The liberation
of the gospel was intended to work like leaven in the meal of
centuries of oppression.

In the beginning it was not so. God revealed his heart when he
created both man and woman in his own image; when he called
Abraham to found a nation through whom *all* nations would be
blessed; when he led his captive people out of slavery in Egypt;
and when he revealed himself to the poor as the Lord the Provider.
Jesus, the Messiah, revealed the true heart of God when he stood
against all the brutal ways man had devised to enslave his fellow
men and women.

What Jesus said about women

So, what did Jesus say about women? Really, he didn't *say* very much,
but he *did* quite a lot. Jesus did not sit down and say 'Now I'm going
to teach you about women', but he lived and spoke in such a way that
we see his meaning in the context of his life and relationships. This is
how we are meant to learn.

Equality

First of all, the ministry of Jesus so clearly shows us an equality
between men and women that, once you notice it, you see
it everywhere[1]. Of course, due to the culture of the day, more
men are recorded as interacting with Jesus in his ministry, but in
Luke's Gospel alone one third of the relationships mentioned are
with women, and overall in the Gospels forty different women are
mentioned in his teaching and contacts. Indeed, we find that much
of Jesus' teaching is put in a deliberate balance.

For instance, in Luke 15 the parable of the lost sheep is followed

---

1 We are indebted to Ruth Tucker and Walter Liefeld for the original insight,
in their book *Daughters of the Church*, Zondervan, 1987.

by the parable of the lost coin. Both depict what God is like - like a woman searching for a valuable coin and like a shepherd, and like the father in the next parable of the prodigal son. One is about a man and one is about a woman, and both represent God, seeking the lost with great zeal, intensity and persistence.

Then in Luke 18 there are two parables about prayer – in the first a widow keeps on and on trying to get an answer from an unjust judge until at last he relents, saying 'this woman has been bashing me under the eye' (literally in the Greek), and so she gets what she is after. The next story is about two men praying, one a Pharisee, a patriotic citizen, who prays, 'God, I thank you that I am not like other men', and lists all his virtues, and the other a tax collector, a quisling, who beats his breast saying 'God be merciful (literally, be propitiated) to me, the sinner!' Jesus says that it was this man that went away justified. So here are two pictures of prayer that God hears and answers, one from a woman and one from a man.

If there are two men in bed and the Lord comes, one will be taken and one left; if there are two women at the mill grinding, one will be taken and one left. Not just men, not just women, but a balance.

The story of the ten virgins with lamps – five wise, five foolish – is intimately bound together grammatically and conceptually with the next story, about servants who are given talents, under the common heading 'the Kingdom is like' (Matthew 25:1). The men go to do business, or not, with the talents and the virgins go, or do not, to the wedding. These two parables are about entering the Kingdom of God - one about women, and one about men.

There is a man who plants a tiny mustard seed that grows into a great tree, followed by a woman putting some leaven into the dough so the bread will rise. Both stories are telling us about the growth of the Kingdom – one with a man, one with a woman.

In Matthew 12, Jesus talks about Jonah, who went to the Ninevites, and then goes on to say 'The Queen of Sheba will rise up with this generation at the judgement and will condemn it', because she came to Solomon to gain wisdom. So we have two pictures, one of a woman and one of a man taking the truth of the Lord to Gentiles, a thousand years before Jesus came.

On another occasion (Luke 20–21), Jesus says two things about the power of money. In the first he warns against the Scribes and Pharisees who exploit and manipulate widows and 'devour' their houses, and in the next comments on a widow putting her only two coins into the offering. Jesus says she has put in more than all the rich people. A man story, a woman story.

Each synoptic Gospel contains the story of the woman who had been bleeding for twelve years and in each case it is interwoven with the story of Jairus and his daughter. A woman in trouble, a man in trouble. There is a story about the prostitutes and the tax collectors going in to the Kingdom of Heaven before the religious and the respectable. Not just the tax collectors getting in first, not just the prostitutes, but women and men together. In John 3, we read about Nicodemus coming by night and Jesus telling him 'except a man is born again he cannot see or enter the Kingdom', followed in John 4 by Jesus talking to the woman of Samaria and telling her about the water of everlasting life.

You see this wonderful balance all the way through the Gospels: Jesus teaching equality in his ministry, both by example and by illustration.

Jesus' Mother

What is inescapable is that Jesus never gave women instructions or exhortations about their domestic duties. His own mother is never seen in a domestic role when she is mentioned in the Gospels. Indeed, she is never seen at home at all after she was visited in her family home by the angel Gabriel. Shortly after the annunciation, she buzzes off to visit Elizabeth in the hill country and seems to travel about a good deal.

When a woman in the crowd listening to Jesus called out, 'Blessed is the womb that bore you and the breasts at which you nursed', (because she could not think of any higher ideal for a woman than to be the mother of the Messiah), Jesus replied: 'On the contrary, blessed are those who hear the word of God and observe it' (Luke 11:27-8). Jesus did not rebuke this woman for speaking publicly[2] – he simply corrected her wrong evaluation of womanhood. (Jesus took remarks made to him by women seriously and did not put women down, even when they were wrong.) Here again Jesus redefines the role of women – the paradigm was not domestic service, nor childbirth, but hearing and following, that is, discipleship. As Jesus was referring to his own mother here, his words are very significant.

Some Christian leaders have found this remark of Jesus problematic. They fear that the perception that Jesus could be giving relatively less importance to the role of motherhood than traditional Judaism did, must result in married women neglecting their children in order to 'serve the Lord'! The evangelist Gypsy Smith once received a letter from a woman telling him that she was called to preach and teach, and asking for his advice as to how to begin. She also mentioned that she had twelve children. He is said to have replied, 'Dear Madam, I am delighted to hear that you are called to preach the gospel. I am even more delighted that God has provided you with a congregation to preach to...'

Of course, we would agree that discipleship begins at home, but this concern about family duties and commitments does not always extend to the father of the family. It is assumed, even today, that the wife will carry the brunt of the responsibility for child-care, etc. Naturally, no-one should overlook their duty to care for their family, since one of the qualifications for church leadership set out by the apostle Paul is that the leader should have well-

---

2 Another woman whom Jesus positively encouraged to speak in public was she who touched the hem of his garment. He made her testify to her healing before the whole crowd.

behaved children (1 Timothy 3:12). It is difficult to raise secure, happy, disciplined children if you are never there, or if you are always emotionally absent.

Women leaders usually take maternity leave from their duty for short or longer periods of time in order to establish their family. This lifts from them some of the spiritual and managerial stress that their role inevitably contains. Of course the physical and emotional stresses of pregnancy, childbirth and lactation can make a woman feel vulnerable in other ways, but most women enjoy the opportunity to literally nurture a new life, and find this different expression of creativity a great joy.

The difficulty often comes with the changed perception a mother has of herself, and in the eyes of others. This formerly confident, capable woman has not only dramatically changed shape over a period of months, but then is constantly accompanied by a needy little person who demands her whole time and attention. This can leave a woman asking herself, 'Who am I?', and others asking, 'Should this busy mother be leading?' No wonder some women find motherhood a confusing time.

Of course, the degree to which these perceptions occur will vary with the nature of the leadership role a person has. Similarly, the time when the demands and stresses of motherhood lessen will also vary widely and unpredictably. No pressure should be put on a mother to return to 'full-time' work and service before she is ready to. On the other hand, no-one should assume she is incapable of resuming her leadership role because she is now exercising her pastoral and maternal gifts on the home-front as well as in the church. As we have seen, the mother of Jesus managed to raise the finest son the world has ever seen, while being totally caught up in the work of God. Mary even 'lost' Jesus when he was only twelve years old on the way home from Jerusalem (Luke 2:41-50). Perhaps because she was so absorbed in discussing the teaching in the Temple with her husband and other pilgrims (of course like many mothers, she scolded her child for her own lapse of vigilance! v48).

Mary and Martha

Martha and Mary are two outstanding women of the Gospels, and are an interesting study in themselves. These two sisters said and did some of the most remarkable things, both about and to Jesus, and give us a fascinating insight into how Jesus viewed and treated women.

It is a traditional interpretation that Mary Magdalene is the same person as Mary of Bethany, who wept at the Lord's feet and anointed Jesus with costly spikenard[3]. Judas and others objected to her extravagant action, but Jesus warned them: 'Why do you bother the woman? For she has done a good deed to me.' Her intuition was that Jesus was going to be crucified, and she anointed him[4] – 'she did it to prepare me for burial.' Jesus then went on to make the amazing pronouncement that 'Wherever this gospel is preached in the whole world, what this woman has done will also be spoken of in memory of her.' This is the highest accolade Jesus ever gave to anyone, male or female. Mary's prophetic action not only showed acute spiritual perception and sensitivity but was the reflection of a deep personal devotion to Jesus Christ which lies at the heart of the Christian life.

Mary saw herself as a disciple of Jesus. In Luke 10 where Martha is distracted by household chores, Mary 'sits at the feet of' Jesus, which in Greek was a technical term denoting discipleship (cf. Acts 22:3, RSV), not simply a description of where she was sitting. Jesus praised her for that choice – 'Mary has chosen the

---

3 John 12:1-8, Matthew 26:6-13

4 It is interesting to note that Christ was only anointed – 'christed' – by women, one being Mary of Bethany, and the other the anonymous forgiven sinner in Luke 7:36-50, who herself displayed unique insight into Jesus' forgiveness.

better part, which will not be taken away from her.' Incidentally, Jesus does not appear to rebuke Martha directly despite her outrageous complaint and demand – perhaps he recognised her outburst as stress-induced!

Nevertheless, Jesus' response to Martha is interesting: first, he begins it with the double vocative, 'Martha, Martha'. There are only seven occasions in Scripture when God uses a person's name twice in this way, and each time a word of deep importance follows[5]. Martha is the only woman among them. Through his words to her, Jesus is pointing out that the role of discipleship Mary has chosen is a better and more enduring one than the domestic role Martha is fulfilling at that moment: Jesus thought it was more important for women to learn than to serve. This revolutionary redefinition of the role of women seems to worry many commentators who rush to assure us that Jesus is not undermining the importance of the domestic role!

In John 11 when Jesus goes to raise their brother, Lazarus, from the dead, Martha is the first to speak to Him. After talking, Jesus says to her, 'I am the resurrection and the life; he who believes in me will live even if he dies, and everyone who lives and believes in me will never die. Do you believe this?' Martha replies, 'Yes, Lord; I have believed that you are the Christ, the Son of God.' This confession is almost identical to the Great Confession, when after Jesus asked 'Who do you say that I am?', Peter said 'You are the Christ, the Son of the living God' (Matthew 16:16). You cannot get a greater confession of faith, and just as it was true for Peter that 'flesh and blood did not reveal this to you, but My Father who is in heaven', it was equally true for Martha[6].

---

5 Cf. Genesis 22:11 – Abraham; Genesis 46:2 – Jacob; Exodus 3:4 – Moses; 1 Samuel 3:10 – Samuel; Luke 22:31 – Simon Peter; Acts 9:4 - Saul.

6 Also, we can hardly escape the fact that Jesus was a lot harder on men than women when they tried to exercise authority over him. 'Out of my sight, Satan! You are a stumbling block to me; for you are not setting your mind on the things of God, but the things of man' (Matthew 16:23) – this to Peter, the 'prince' of the apostles, just after the Great Confession.

Mary Magdalene was the first person to whom the risen Jesus revealed himself and the first eyewitness to the Gospel. It is remarkable, given that women were not allowed to testify in court, that it was Mary who was entrusted with the good news of Jesus' resurrection when she was sent to tell the other disciples. Mary was the first apostle of the resurrection (1 Corinthians 15), and because of this the Early Church Fathers referred to her as the Apostle to the apostles – the Apostle squared!

So, just as in John's Gospel Martha was the female counterpart of the confession of Christ seen in the Synoptic Gospels, Mary was the first person to testify of the risen Lord Jesus. Martha and Mary stand out as two women exalted by Jesus, and in themselves represent the whole gospel.

Honoured and exalted

There is such a beauty in Christ – not just in what he taught but in the way he lived it himself. Not only does Jesus' ministry embody equality, it demonstrates particular respect and honour for women.

In John 19, during the crucifixion Jesus sees his mother, and, despite almost unendurable physical, emotional and spiritual torment – added to which the burden of the consequences of the world's rebellion, sin and hostility against God – incredibly he says 'Woman, behold your son', and to John, 'son behold your mother!' Through all the pain and humiliation, Jesus took his mother into account, honouring her and providing for her. Jesus honoured his mother, not just in order to obey the Law, or because of her unique role in mothering the Messiah, which would have been a source of envy for many women, but as we noted above, because she had heard God's word and kept it: 'Blessed is she who believed that there would be a fulfilment of what had been spoken to her by the Lord' (Luke 1:45).

Not only did Jesus talk to Jewish women but, even more controversially, to Gentile women too. In John 4, we see the disciples are amazed that Jesus is talking to the woman at the well, because no rabbi ever would, and would not even speak to their wives in public. But Jesus crossed those barriers, ignored the political correctness, sat down and talked to her. Even though he tells her that he knows she has had five husbands and now has another she has not even bothered to marry, there was not the slightest hint of condemnation in that conversation. Instead, she asks a theological question, which Jesus took seriously and answered. His heart went out to her and he wanted to see her drawing water from the well of water springing up to everlasting life – and she became an effective evangelist.

Nor does Jesus condemn the woman brought to him caught in the act of adultery, as part of an attempt to trick him into breaking the Law of Moses (John 8). While there was no question of her guilt, Jesus said 'he that is without sin cast the first stone', and they all went out one by one. 'No-one condemns you?' he said, 'neither do I condemn you', and in so doing kept the Law, because he was not an eye-witness, and could not be an accuser. At the same time his overwhelming desire was that she entered into a fuller, fresher, divine life that was going to bring her fulfilment and satisfaction - 'Go and sin no more'. That is why he talked to her, that's why he took the trouble to salvage her from the hands of religious fanatics who wanted to destroy her.

He also saw a woman crippled by Satan for eighteen years and took the trouble to release her – 'should not this daughter of Abraham be set free?' What good would she do for the Kingdom? She was a nobody, but she was a victim of Satan. Sinners, victims of Satan – women can be both and they need releasing and delivering.

The proclamation of the gospel

The linking of Mary of Bethany with the gospel that will be 'preached throughout the world' is very striking. It is not the only place where women are significantly linked to the proclamation of the good news.

Quite apart from the women who travelled with Jesus, witnessing most of his miracles and hearing most of his teaching, women were also key witnesses to his death and resurrection.

When Jesus was about to return to the Father, he instructed his disciples to wait in Jerusalem until they received 'power from on high' (Luke 24:49). This power would enable them to be witnesses to Jesus, in particular to his resurrection. It is not surprising, therefore, that those who were able to bear witness most fully to his resurrection were the women who had so devotedly followed him.

They saw and heard more of the supernatural events surrounding the resurrection than the male disciples did. It may be true that, at the time, they ran less risk in going to the tomb than the men did, but that can have little to do with God's choosing to unfold before them some of the astonishing incidents, and making them the principal witnesses to the drama. He later required other disciples to witness the empty tomb, in spite of the risk to their safety. But it was the women who saw the guards lying in fear like dead men, the stone rolled away and an angel sitting on it. They were also spoken to by angels. It was first to Mary Magdalene that Jesus appeared after he had risen, and second to the other women, and he commanded them to take the news of his resurrection and coming ascension to the other disciples.

There is something powerfully significant about the fact that women were first commanded to proclaim the resurrection of Jesus. These women were almost certainly present on the day of Pentecost, when the Holy Spirit came to empower them all to be witnesses. On that occasion Peter quoted from the prophet Joel that God's servants, both men and women, would prophesy. All this was a further fulfilment of Psalm 68:11, which, unlike many translations, the NASB correctly translates: 'The Lord gives the command; the women who proclaim the good tidings are a great host.' A prophecy manifestly fulfilled by the vast numbers of women who later participated on the mission field.

So that is what Jesus thought about women – they are equal,

they are honoured and they are exalted by him. Here is how Dorothy L Sayers, detective author and theologian, summed it up:

> Perhaps it is no wonder that the women were the first at the cradle and last at the cross. They had never known a man like this man; there never has been such another. A prophet and a teacher who never nagged at them, never flattered or coaxed or patronised; who never made arch jokes about them, never treated them either as 'The women, God help us!' Or 'The ladies, God bless them!'; who rebuked without querulousness and praised without condescension; who took their questions and arguments seriously; who never mapped out their sphere for them to be feminine or jeered at them for being female, who had no axe to grind or no uneasy male dignity to defend; who took them as he found them and was completely unselfconscious.[7]

The male apostles

There is only one issue on which Jesus has been charged with sex discrimination, and that is in his choice of twelve male apostles. No theological reason is given in the text in terms of men's supposed superiority of authority and intellect. Suggestions have been made in order to find reasons for Jesus' choice, namely that:

i   Jesus was accommodating to the prejudices of his day. Knowing that the people would not listen to a woman, he pragmatically appoints men

ii Jesus knew that mankind for all generations would belittle womanhood and so gives a guide for future church leadership

iii No woman of Jesus' day would have known the Scriptures well enough to be a definitive teacher of the 'apostolic' doctrine.

---

7 Dorothy L Sayers, *Are Women Human?* (Grand Rapids: Eerdmans, 1971)

While these ideas may have some bearing on the situation, they hardly seem weighty enough if we believe that Jesus is showing us truth for all time. Such cultural considerations would surely be irrelevant for future Church generations to come – Jesus did not appoint a slave or a gentile among the twelve, just as he did not appoint a woman (see chapter 3, pp 24-26).

However, there is a symbolic consideration in the appointment of the twelve. Everyone in Jesus' day would see the significance of twelve new patriarchs forming a new Israel. Jesus was challenging the old order, and twelve men – the disciples – would be a clear sign to the old people of God that a new nation was coming into being in place of Israel and the twelve original patriarchs (Matthew 21:43).

The twelve alone participated in the Last Supper, but no one has ever thought, either in the Early Church or since, that women should be excluded when we 'do this in remembrance of him'. Consequently the exclusion of women from an apostolate should not be a foregone conclusion either.

If Jesus is symbolizing a new people of God in the choice of twelve men, then no inference can be drawn from, nor can an anti-feminist attitude be read into, this one seemingly discriminating act of Jesus. He who washed feet (John 13:5), made breakfast (John 21:12), taught his male disciples to wait upon people (Luke 9:16) and cuddled infants (Luke 18:15) – all 'feminine' activities – is not likely to disparage womanhood or discriminate against his female disciples. For Jesus, women were and are human beings, having a full place in his Kingdom.

Deity and femininity

Among some Christians today some confusion appears to persist over the concept of sexuality and God, like the little girl who wrote in a letter to God, 'Are boys better than girls? I know you are one, but try to be fair, Love Sylvie.' Does anyone seriously believe that God is a sexual being in a physical sense? Perhaps he is both masculine and feminine at heart: fifty per cent masculine and fifty per cent feminine. Jesus said that in the resurrection there will be no marriage, but that we will be 'as the angels', who are presumably 'asexual' like God himself.

It is clearly erroneous to equate maleness – in human terms – with God: it is to make God a man. Rather, since God made both male and female in his image (Genesis 1:26), we may reasonably deduce that masculinity and femininity are both contained in God's nature, as indeed they are in ours: while being male in terms of gender, men embody what we might identify as more feminine characteristics, such as the ability to respond to initiative, to nurture and to trust themselves to another; to create from the intuitive and feeling part of themselves, to be tender and simply to 'be'. Women, while female in gender, exhibit 'masculine' qualities: from the rational, 'doing' mind they initiate, critique, shape, direct, bring order and pierce through difficulty.[8]

At times too heavy an emphasis has been placed on the male as representing the divine, which is a questionable notion at best: the woman of wisdom in Proverbs chapter 8 equally represents the divine. Jesus sees himself as Wisdom (Matthew 11:19, as does Paul in 1 Corinthians 1:30), drawing from this female image. Perhaps this is why Jesus is seen with female breasts in Revelation 1:13[9]. Some people have such an abhorrence of linking femininity with God that they cannot accept that this vision of Jesus could depict his nurturing his people with the milk of the word.

---

8 See Leanne Payne's *Crisis in Masculinity* and *Restoring the Christian Soul* (both published by Kingsway) for more on the subject of the true masculine and true feminine. See also chapter 12, *Masculinity and Femininity*

9 While it would not be unheard-of for a first-century Greek to use this word to mean a male chest, it is only used in relation to a woman in the two other New Testament uses of it, and another Greek word is used elsewhere in Revelation for a male 'chest'. In either case it must be remembered that it is a symbol, as is the white hair and the sword in place of a tongue also seen in this vision.

It is possible to speak of God using female as well as male symbols. God explicitly describes himself in female terms in a number of passages (Isaiah 42:14; 46:3; 49:15). Moreover, God represents himself as a mother in Isaiah 66:13. Jesus likened God to a woman sweeping a room. He also said that, like a hen, the Son would gather the people of Jerusalem like chicks under her wings. Although grammatical gender does not always correspond to the male or female sex, it may not be insignificant that the Hebrew word for 'spirit' – *ruach* – and the Greek word for 'dove' – *peristera* – used as a symbol of the Holy Spirit, are both feminine.

To suggest to women that in the resurrection they will become male in order to be like God, while men remain as they are, is to reduce femininity to a temporal aberration, neither fully human nor divine. The suggestion is reminiscent of Eastern religions, where women, believed to be a lower species, might hope to attain maleness through reincarnation. This is not to say that we are at liberty to change the name of God, that wonderful name 'Father', nor to worship him as a goddess. We worship neither a man nor a woman on the throne of the universe, nor some kind of bisexual being, but a God who created both, along with their sexuality. Jesus was certainly incarnated as a male, but the God who indwells us by his Holy Spirit is at once perfectly masculine and perfectly feminine. It is interesting to note that the Holy Spirit in an aggressive person will make them more gentle in spirit, while the Holy Spirit in those of a fearful disposition puts steel into them, giving them courage and endurance. God desires to make us whole people, not 'macho' males nor 'fluffy' females, but men and women worthy of the eternal destiny he has for us.

In fact, it could be argued that as Christians, we must pursue 'biblical personhood', rather than models of 'biblical manhood and womanhood' – a dubious concept anyway, since much of the material written about these 'models' is drawn from difficult and controversial texts, and has no support whatever in the teaching of Jesus. The call to discipleship in the New Testament is no respecter of gender; and its high standards and stringent demands offer enough material for discussion, debate and reflection to last a lifetime.

Conclusion

It has rightly been pointed out that Jesus' relationships with women were unique in the annals of religious history and in stark contrast to the attitudes of Jewish rabbis of his day. Jesus travelled with women (Luke 8:1-3), a practice which, in his day, bordered on the outrageous. Jesus healed women both physically and spiritually. Jesus taught women both privately and publicly, and had disciples who were women, who sat at his feet and heard his word. He talked to women: the only person to whom Jesus revealed himself personally as the Christ was the Samaritan woman, one of the two people commended for 'great faith' is a woman (Matthew 15:28) and he reserved his highest praise for a woman (Matthew 26:13). While Jesus did not say that women should teach or lead, he certainly did not give commands to women not to teach or lead.

Because of his deity, Jesus combines the best of femininity and the best of masculinity, perfectly balanced in his person. Of course, if you lose sight of Jesus, it isn't very long before you lose that equality, and sadly this can be seen throughout Church history right through to today.

5

The Use of Gifts

In Romans 16:1-2 we read of Phoebe, who is called a '*diakonos*', translated as servant, deacon or minister. She is also said to be a '*prostatis*', that is,'helper' or 'succourer'. Both of these occur in the list of spiritual gifts found in Romans 12:6-8. *Diakonos* is used twenty-two times in the New Testament and is always masculine, even though here it is applied to a woman. This will have bearing on other words such as 'elder', which, as we will discuss in chapter 6, may appear to be exclusively masculine in form, but inclusive of females in practice. Conversely, *prostatis* is in the feminine form and means 'one who stands before', 'a chief', 'leader of a party', 'protector' or 'champion'[1].

Throughout the Bible we can find examples of women using spiritual gifts. The New Testament teaches that spiritual gifts are given to the individual believer by the Holy Spirit for the building up of the Church, and each gift carries authority and responsibility. In Romans 12 Paul gives one list of gifts, which we show here, and beside each gift we reference the women seen exercising it in

---

1 The corresponding verb is used in 1 Thessalonians 5:12, 1 Timothy 5:17 and Romans 12:8.

the Bible. It is worth noting, that not only are there examples in Scripture of women as well as men using each of these gifts, there are also no direct prohibitions against women exercising authority in these gifts or in any formal leadership role.

Gifts listed in Romans chapter 12:

Prophecy: Miriam (Exodus 15:20)
     Deborah (Judges 4:4)
     Huldah (2 Chronicles 34:22-28)
     Isaiah's wife (Isaiah 8:3)
     Anna (Luke 2:36-8)
     Philip's daughters (Acts 21:9)

Service or helps: Rufus's mother (Romans 16:13)
     Lydia (Acts 16:15)
     Priscilla (Acts 18:3)

Teaching: Priscilla (Acts 18:24-6)
    Deborah (4:5)

Encouragement: Elizabeth (Luke 1:41-5)

Giving: The women who ministered to Jesus (Luke 8:1-3)
   The Widow's mite (Mark 12:42-3)

Leadership: Miriam (Micah 6:4)
    Deborah (Judges 4:4)
    Phoebe (Romans 16:2)

Showing mercy: Dorcas (Acts 9:39)

In 1 Corinthians 12 Paul gives another list of gifts, known as the charismatic gifts: Wisdom, Knowledge, Healings, Miracles, Discernment of Spirits and Tongues. These charismatic gifts were not confined to men. Women were also present on the day of Pentecost (Acts 1:14; 2:4) and the Spirit was poured out on them (Acts 2:17-18). In Mark 16 'those who have believed' (v17) is an inclusive pronoun, including women as well as men, which meant that they could be equipped with the power for casting out demons, for speaking in tongues and for healing.

A third list of gifts, the ministry gifts, appears in Ephesians 4. We understand these ministries to be the embodiment of a charismatic gift in a person. The five-fold ministry of the Church comprises the following:

Ministry gifts listed in Ephesians 4:

Apostle: Junia (Romans 16:7)

Prophet: Deborah (Judges 5:7,12)
        Isaiah's wife (Isaiah 8:3)
        Philip's daughters (Acts 21:9)

Evangelist: The woman at the well (John 4:28-30,39)
        Euodia, Syntyche (Philippians 4:2)
        The great company of women (Psalm 68:11)

Pastor/teacher: 'Women Deacons' (1 Timothy 3:11)
        Older women (Titus 2:3-5)

Conclusion

Much more could and has been written about women's gifts in the Church, but hopefully this condensed account will encourage women to grow and mature in the faith of Jesus Christ and to find the areas of gifting God wants to release them in.

In this section we have demonstrated a consistent treatment of women by the Trinitarian God. God made men and women equally in his image, and in the Old Testament gave women spiritual authority and leadership responsibility, as we saw in chapters 1 and 2. Jesus, reflecting the Father's heart treated women as full human beings with honour and respect, as we saw in chapter 4. To complete the Trinitarian overview, in this chapter we see that the Holy Spirit equally infills women and men and gives spiritual gifts and ministries to both. Father, Son and Holy Spirit all welcome the fullest participation of women in their kingdom.

6

Paul in Context

Following Paul

As Christians, we 'follow the Lamb wherever he goes' (Revelation 14:4, Ephesians 5:1). We also follow Paul, as he too follows Christ (1 Corinthians 11:1, 1 Timothy 1:16). It is important that we do not make Paul contradict Christ, because if we do then we have misunderstood him. Some religions, such as Islam use the principle of abrogation, that is, earlier texts are invalidated by later texts that appear to be contradictory. However, Jesus affirms the opposite – earlier texts take precedence for interpretation. For example, on divorce Jesus says 'from the beginning it has not been this way.'[1] Paul follows this precedent in Galatians 3:17;

> the Law, which came four hundred and thirty years
> later, does not invalidate a covenant previously ratified
> by God, so as to nullify the promise.

The Law must be understood in the light of Abraham's promise and not vice versa. In the same way Jesus made it clear he came to

---

1   Matthew 19:3-9 referring to Genesis 2, cf. Matthew 5:17

build on the Law, not to destroy it (Matthew 5:17), even if he had to reinterpret it. Therefore, Paul must be understood in the light of what Jesus taught in the Gospels and not be made to contradict that, the work of the Spirit in Acts, or indeed the Old Testament.

We have already seen that Jesus is the great emancipator of disadvantaged womankind and in no way restricts female involvement in the kingdom. So, what then are we to make of the two passages in Paul's epistles that seem to place restrictions on women in the Church? In order to begin, we need to set down some basic principles of how we interpret what Paul says.

Principles of interpretation

The interpretation of any biblical text has to be based on firm principles. There are four in particular we will use here: translation, integrity, Christ-centredness and cultural and literary context.

Translation

Greek texts were written as lines of letters with no spaces between words, no punctuation marks and no sentences or paragraphs[2]. All of our modern translations have these things added in.

Because languages involve symbolic representations of concepts as words, translation inherently involves interpretation, especially where directly equivalent words or phrases are not available, or carry different nuances. Grammatical differences between languages lead to changes, especially to improve the flow[3]. In addition, doctrinal bias in translating can result in significant textual differences in the translation, especially over ambiguous, difficult or rare words. For example, the Hebrew particle *nā'* appears over 60 times in the Old Testament and is translated as 'please' or 'I beg you' except for the five occasions when God says

---

2 The 'chapter and verse' systematic division scheme of the Bible was devised by Stephen Langton in the thirteenth century.

3 Some translations, such as the NASB, show in italics where words have been added in that are not present in the original text.

nā', where it is just omitted from most translations[4]. If you think God is omnipotent, or predestines everything, he would never say 'please' to anyone, in which case it is far more comfortable to pretend he doesn't and ignore it. This is a small example of a much bigger problem with historical theological bias in modern translations[5]. For meaningful interpretation we must try to ensure that what we read in our translations reflects the original text as closely as possible.

Integrity

Our second principle is that the Bible will not contradict itself. The interpretation of one passage should not go against other statements in the Bible on the same matter, or our overall understanding of the Scriptures. On the issue of women in leadership, how can we make the leadership examples of Miriam, Huldah, Deborah, Sarah and Priscilla, sit well with 1 Timothy 2:12?

Apparent contradictions in the Bible sometimes require complex exegesis to unravel them so as to preserve the integrity of the Scriptures. For example, the story of David numbering Israel (2 Samuel 24:1 and 1 Chronicles 21:1), where both God and Satan are presented as the causes of this event respectively. We can understand this apparent contradiction in that God is the ultimate cause of everything, and here Satan was the immediate cause.

Second, in Mark 10:46 Bartimaeus is healed by Jesus as he leaves Jericho, but in Luke 18:35, it says it was when he was entering the city. Possibly this is because there was an 'old' and a 'new' city of Jericho, that is, the whole city was in two parts.

Third, justification is by faith according to Galatians 2:16, but by works according to James 2:25, but these works are not works of the law, as in Romans 3:20, but works of faith (James 2:22-3).

---

4 Genesis 13:14, 15:5; 22:2; Exodus 11:12, Isaiah 7:3. See V Hamilton, *The Book of Genesis*, (NICONT, Eerdman, 1988)

5 For more on this subject please see *God's Strategy in Human History*, by Roger Forster and Paul Marston

So too, complex and careful exegesis is necessary here to avoid making 1 Corinthians 11–14 and 1 Timothy 2 contradict Paul's other writings and the rest of Scripture.

Similarly, no significant doctrine should rest on one passage of Scripture alone in accordance with the principle that in the mouth of two or three witnesses a thing should be established (2 Corinthians 13:1).

Christ-centredness

Different people read the Bible in different ways – Jews, Jehovah's Witnesses, Muslims and secular analysts read the Bible and interpret it with different paradigms. As Christians, we must understand the teaching of the Old Testament and the Epistles in light of the historical Jesus of the gospels, as all of God's words lead to and come together in the Word (cf. John 5:39-40; Luke 24:27). This is known as a Christo-centric or a Christological hermeneutic.

As a Pharisee, Saul knew the Hebrew Scriptures well, reading and interpreting them as a Jew in the original language. Following his conversion Paul interpreted the Old Testament in the light of the gospel, clearly placing Christ at the centre of his understanding. As such, Paul's practice is unlikely to differ from that of Jesus.

Cultural and literary context

Each passage of Scripture must be understood in its historical and cultural situation before applying it to our own. The Song of Solomon is hardly to be understood and applied in the same way as Deuteronomy or 1 Chronicles.

This is especially important when understanding Paul's writing, much of which was written to directly address very specific needs and conditions which he had heard about or was asked to give guidance on. Paul answered these needs, taking the cultural contexts of the individual churches into account, using language, analogies, symbols and references that they would understand. While Paul sometimes gives commands from the Lord, at other times he says, 'I have no commandment from the Lord', and gives direction which is his wisdom for the time (1 Corinthians 7:6,25).

1 Timothy 5:23, Galatians 5:12 and 1 Corinthians 7:7 should be warnings to us not to elevate Paul's personal asides and wisdom to the same level as our Lord's commands and the Holy Spirit's injunctions through Paul, Peter and other New Testament writers[6]. Proverbs 30:33 is Scripture but not of the same order and authority as Exodus 20:13-14! In 1 Timothy 2:9-12, Paul is very clear that he is not invoking our Lord's authority, but giving us *his* scripturally illustrated wisdom to meet a specific need. When this need is understood, we can apply the truth for ourselves, and it can be useful to ask 'what is the question Paul is answering?'

Literary context is also an important consideration and comprises the surrounding passages, their themes, flow and development of ideas, as well as any other Scripture that a passage refers to, or is referred to by. For example, if a passage concerning men and women refers to Genesis 1, it is most likely referring to male and female in general, whereas if it refers to Genesis 2 it is husbands and wives that are in view.

Overview of Paul

From his conversion circa 36AD until his death in around 67AD Paul travelled thousands of miles on missionary work accompanied by many co-workers, planted and oversaw many new churches and wrote many letters of teaching and encouragement. The timeline overleaf shows an approximate scheme of important events in Paul's life relevant to the letters of 1 Corinthians and 1 Timothy.

6 The apostles and elders in Jerusalem did not add a new doctrine for the Church for all time when they said, in Acts 15:28, 'For it seemed good to the Holy Spirit and to us to lay upon you no greater burden than these essentials ...' This guidance was born out of their corporate wisdom in the Holy Spirit, for the immediate situation in Antioch, Syria and Cilicia

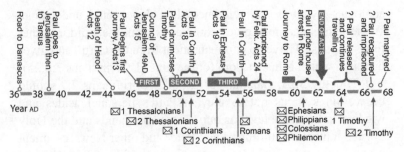

Timeline of events in Paul's ministry

Background to 1 Corinthians

Corinth

Corinth was a cosmopolitan port positioned at the intersection of trade routes between Asia to the east and Rome to the west. With its two large harbours and command of the isthmus it was an important stop for sailors, merchants and commercial travellers.

Ancient Corinth had become synonymous with sexual vice since the fourth century BC. For example, Aristophanes used *korinthiazomai* (I live as a Corinthian) as a neologism for drunken and immoral debauchery, and Plato used the term *korinthia kore* (girl from Corinth) to mean prostitute. However, this was not the same Corinth Paul visited, as the old city was destroyed in 146BC, and rebuilt and repopulated under Julius Caesar in 44BC, including many freedmen (released slaves) from Rome. In the new city, just as in any other major Greek city, prostitution was a widespread and visible industry, even more so given the large passing trade. Archaeologists excavating Cornith discovered 33 wine shops on a single street, which, allied with its reputation for promiscuity and the direct warnings given by Paul in 1 Corinthians 6 16-20, indicates that sexual and drunken debauchery were a significant part of Corinthian life that could not be overlooked.

Corinth was home to the Isthmia Games – second only to the Olympics, which were not just an athletic event, but dedicated to the gods, chief among which was the Roman Emperor. As such Corinth became a centre of the Imperial Cult. In 1 Corinthians Paul alludes not only to the Isthmia Games (9:24-27), but also to the cultural pressures that existed to attend banquets honouring the Emperor as well as other gods, which would be attended by Greek men accompanied by heterae and flute girls (see page 59). There were numerous temples in Corinth, including ones dedicated to Poseidon, the god of the sea, Asklepios, Apollo, Hermes, Venus-Fortuna, Isis and a Pantheon dedicated to all the gods. But the biggest temple was that of Aphrodite (Venus to the Romans) the patron goddess of love, sexuality and prostitutes.

While, historical reports of 1000 courtesans serving in the temple of Aphrodite may be exaggerated, many temples owned prostitutes which they used as a source of income.

The Corinthian Church

Paul first visited Corinth on his second missionary journey (Acts 18), where he met Aquila and Priscilla who had been expelled from Rome (circa 49AD). After being rejected by the Jews, Paul preached to the Gentiles and started a church in the house next door to the synagogue. The leader of the synagogue, Crispus, became a believer, as did many Corinthians, but the Jews conspired to have Paul imprisoned by Gallio, the proconsul of Achaia (51-52AD), but were dismissed. After eighteen months in Corinth Paul left for Syria with Priscilla and Aquila.

Paul wrote at least four letters to the church in Corinth, of which 1 Corinthians is the second, written in response to a letter he received from them. From the people Paul refers to, the church appears to have been composed of a mixture of Romans, Jews and Greeks, slaves and free (1 Corinthians 12:13), and as such was like a miniature version of the city.

It is clear from the content of 1 Corinthians that divisions had arisen both between Paul and the church as well as internal factions within the church (1 Corinthians 1:10-12, 3:4-5, 11:18-19). During his three year stay in Ephesus, Paul sent Timothy to Corinth to teach and instruct them. Paul then made 'a painful visit' to Corinth (2 Corinthians 2:1) and on his return to Ephesus wrote a 'sorrowful letter' (2:4, 7:8) before writing 2 Corinthians, probably in Philippi on his way back to Jerusalem.

Background to 1 Timothy

Ephesus

Ephesus was the Roman capital of Asia Minor and was the third largest city in the Empire, behind Rome and Constantinople. Like Corinth, Ephesus was the major port in its region, drawing merchants and travellers from across the known world. Ephesus was also a centre of cult pilgrimage to the Temple of Artemis, which was one of Herodotus' Seven Wonders of the Ancient World. Artemis was originally a virgin goddess of wild animals and hunting, but the Ephesians formerly worshipped Cybele, the earth mother goddess, who represented fertility. Over time the rituals and beliefs of the two were syncretically assimilated in the temple of Artemis, giving rise to the cult of Ephesian Artemis which, like Cybele, was served in the temple by slave women under the direction of a priestess attended by eunuch priests and young virgins.

The Church in Ephesus

After leaving Corinth Paul went to Ephesus with Aquila and Priscilla, but although the Jews asked him to stay he moved on, promising to return 'if God wills' (Acts 18:21). Aquila and Priscilla remained in Ephesus, where they instructed Apollos when he arrived before he then travelled to Corinth.

On his third missionary journey Paul spent three years in Ephesus. On the way there he encountered twelve disciples of Apollos whom he baptised in water and the Spirit. Just as in Corinth, Paul preached in the synagogue until the Jews rejected him and then preached to the Gentiles, resulting in the Ephesian church being made up of a mixture of Jews and Greeks. Many miracles were happening at Ephesus and the church had such a significant impact that idol makers, led by Demetrius, staged an uprising in protest at lost trade and the threat to the temple of Artemis itself as a place of global importance (Acts 19:23-41).

It is an Early Church tradition that the apostle John and Jesus' mother Mary moved to Ephesus and were involved in the church there. Paul's letter to the Ephesians was most likely written during his house arrest in Rome. In 1 Timothy 1:3 we see that Paul instructed Timothy to remain in Ephesus, but given the journeys he refers to, this happened after Paul was released from prison in Rome. The situation in Ephesus was similar to that in Corinth, where different doctrines were invading the church and divisions were arising.

Timothy

Timothy is first mentioned in Acts 16:1 when Paul and Barnabas pass through Lystra and Derbe on the second missionary journey. Both his mother and grandmother – Eunice and Lois – were Jewish converts and his father was Greek. Already a believer, Timothy's reputation had spread and he was chosen by Paul as a new co-worker. Paul circumcised Timothy so he would be able to witness to both Jews and Gentiles, and together with Silas they set off for Macedonia.

Given the paternal language Paul uses about Timothy[7] he may even have led him to the Lord on the first missionary journey. Either way, Paul saw Timothy as a gifted teacher and preacher (2 Corinthians 1:19), a fellow worker (Romans 16:21, 1 Thessalonians 3:2) a bond-servant (Philippians 1:1) and listed him as co-author of 2 Corinthians, Philippians, Colossians, 1

---

7 See 1 Corinthians 4:17; 1 Timothy 1:2,18; 2 Timothy 1:2; Philippians 2:19-24

Thessalonians, 2 Thessalonians and Philemon.

Paul had faith in Timothy to represent him and his apostleship over the churches – 'I have no one else of kindred spirit who will genuinely be concerned for your welfare' (Philippians 2:20). On a number of occasions Paul left him in, or sent him into, difficult and potentially dangerous situations. For example, in Acts 17 when Paul had to flee the Thessalonian Jews he left Timothy and Silas to instruct the new converts in Berea. When Paul was in Athens he sent Timothy to Thessalonica to teach and encourage them in the face of persecution (1 Thessalonians 3:1-3).

Paul probably wrote both 1 and 2 Corinthians duing his three year stay in Ephesus. After hearing of the contentious situation in Corinth, with sin rampant and his apostolic authority in question, Paul wrote 1 Corinthians and sent Timothy to instruct them. Following Timothy's return Paul wrote 2 Corinthians where Timothy is included in the salutation. Timothy had first visited the Church in Corinth on the second missionary journey where he and Silas were reunited with Paul (Acts 18:5) and brought good news from the Thessalonians (1 Thessalonians 3:6). All three were then based in Corinth for eighteen months, during which time Paul probably wrote 1 and 2 Thessalonians, which are ascribed to all three. It is likely that Timothy then accompanied Paul to Ephesus on the second missionary journey, but he certainly stayed there at some time during the third journey (Acts 19:22).

Timothy ministered to Paul during his imprisonment in Rome, and evidently ended up in Ephesus to instruct the church. 1 Timothy was probably written around fifteen years after Paul circumcised Timothy, for significant portions of which they were together. In 2 Timothy 3:10 Paul says 'you have followed my teaching, conduct, purpose, faith, patience, love, perseverance, persecutions and sufferings', and it is clear that Timothy knew and fully understood Paul's theology. If Paul never allowed women to speak or have authority in church Timothy surely would have picked this up after so long. As such, we must assume that any guidance Paul gives in 1 and 2 Timothy must be to do with new problems arising out of specific local theological or practical situations.

Women in Ancient Corinth and Ephesus

Before we look at what Paul said about women, let us briefly look at how women, both Jewish and Greek, were viewed and treated by the cultures in Corinth and Ephesus.

In ancient Greece women were considered as inferior – they could not vote or speak publicly. Marriages were arranged and unmarried women of high status had male relatives as guardians. The remaining unmarried women were either slaves, street prostitutes or heterae (courtesans), who were sophisticated escorts and prostitutes. Heterae were allowed into the Symposia where the men went to talk and attend feasts, but where no wife could enter. Often educated, heterae were intelligent and allowed to speak in public, whereas wives were constrained to the home where their main roles were childbearing and doing domestic chores. Due to their high fees heterae were able to spend money on their appearance, clothing, jewellery and make-up, that other women could not.

Both in Judea and in the communities scattered around the Near East, Jewish women had similar status to Greek women – they were not allowed to testify in court, or speak in public, but were expected to stay at home. The Talmud contains a number of religious laws known as Tzniut pertaining to modest conduct, including rules on dress for Jewish women.

Men were not allowed to listen to women sing, as 'a woman's voice is filthy nakedness', or to talk in public to or spend time with women who were not family members. In the Old Testament, women certainly sang in public worship (1 Chronicles 25:5-6) and Hannah was thought drunk when she prayed silently rather than audibly when at the tabernacle (1 Samuel 1:12-14). Miriam prophesied in answer to Moses' song (Exodus 15:20-21) and was called a prophet.

In Paul's day, women were expected to dress modestly, substantially covering their bodies and avoiding wearing eye-catching colours, especially bright red. Jewish women tied their hair up on their wedding day, and were never seen in public after that without their 'wedding symbol', which the Torah states is a biblical requirement under the Law of Moses (Numbers 5:18). One such pious Jewish woman claimed that even the beams of the ceiling had never seen her head uncovered. Common hair coverings included headscarves or veils. The Old Testament gives no indication that women covered their hair other than for ornamentation – if anything, long flowing locks and braids were seen as beautiful (Song of Solomon 4:1, 6:5, 7:5; Isaiah 3:24). However, in Jewish communities Talmudic teachings made wearing head coverings an inviolable custom, and breaking this law could incur a large fine and was sufficient grounds for divorce.

The Talmud also dictates that Jewish men should 'cover your head in order that the fear of heaven may be upon you.' This was inferred from Exodus 3:6 where 'Moses hid his face, for he was afraid to look at God,' and as such Jewish men had to cover their heads during prayer. It is likely that such rules grew out of the necessity to wear head coverings for protection from the sun, but these became cultural symbols, especially in exiled communities, to distinguish themselves from others. Religious meanings were then attributed to these practices to maintain a sense of distinction.

There were no such rules about hair coverings for Greek women, and while many men and women would wear head coverings for protection or to hold their hair in place, the evidence indicates that worship in Greek temples was done with uncovered heads.

What Paul said about women

Paul has acquired a reputation for holding severe views with regard to women. As a Pharisee, Saul would have adhered to the Talmudic teachings and refused to speak to women, including his own relatives in public (and certainly not Gentiles), and would never have received hospitality in a woman's house. However, after his conversion Paul seems to completely reject these cultural regulations and talked to women – Jew and Gentile – alike in public, stayed in their homes, journeyed with them and exalted them. In short, Paul became just like Jesus.

Let us look at some examples of what Paul said about particular women and womankind in general, and how he treated women – this should help throw light on his attitude.

Apostles

In Romans 16:7 Paul refers to Junia as an apostle. Some recent commentators find it difficult to accept that Junia was female because of the implications, and suggest it must be a masculine contraction of another name. However, Chrysostom – an Early Church Father whose mother tongue was Greek – had no such problem, and wrote: 'Oh how great is the devotion of this woman that she should be even counted worthy of the appellation of apostle.' Paul mentions Andronicus and Junia together as his 'relatives'[8], that is, Jews, and as having been converted before him, over twenty-five years previously. The description of them together – one male and one female name – is indicative of a married couple, which is how it was understood in the Early Church, rather than of two men.

While Paul is not referring to Junia as one of the twelve, she is counted in one of the other categories of apostleship present in the New Testament Church, each of which carried authority.

Ministers

In Romans 16:1-2 Phoebe is called a 'minister' or 'deacon' (sometimes translated 'servant'), a term which Paul also uses to describe Jesus in Romans 15:8, and himself in 1 Corinthians 3:5. While the Greek word *diakonos* is a masculine term, which means the servant of a king, it obviously can be used to describe a woman,

---

8 The word 'men' is not present in the Greek here, which some translators have carelessly added, e.g. as 'kinsmen'. Cranfield's erudite International Critical Commentary book (*Romans*, vol. 2, p.788) comes to the same conclusion.

and as such denotes an office, not a sex.

This has a bearing on the requirements of an elder *(presbuteros)*, which again is a masculine word in Greek that defines an office, but which similarly does not preclude women from filling that position. This is relevant to the issue found in some denominations which inconsistently allow women ministers but not women bishops *(episkopous)*, or overseers as the word means (cf. Acts 20:17,28).

Fellow-workers

Paul uses the term 'fellow worker' to describe Priscilla in Romans 16:3-5. The term is equally used for Aquila, her husband[9], and elsewhere for Timothy (Romans 16:21), Apollos (1 Corinthians 3:6-9) and Clement (Philippians 4:2-3), as well as for two more women – Euodia and Syntyche. Priscilla and Aquila remained in Ephesus to instruct the believers and taught (literally 'exactly expounded' in the Greek) Apollos *together* (Acts 18:26). As they may well have still been present when 1 Timothy was written, it is very unlikely that Paul would then restrict the teaching ministry to male elders only. In the remainder of Romans 16:1-16, in which one third of the people mentioned by name are women, Mary, Tryphena, Tryphosa and Persis are said to be workers who work. The two terms used here for work – *synergeō* and *kopiaō* – are also used by Paul in 1 Corinthians 16:15-16 – 'I urge you, brothers ... to submit to such as these and to everyone who fellow-works and labours'. This must imply we are to submit to female workers, and not merely to males. It is true that the words 'such as these' are either masculine or neuter, but it is gratuitous to insert 'men' into the text as the NASB does, implying those to be submitted to are only male.

Church leaders

Nympha, mentioned in Colossians 4:15, appears to be the leader of a church that met in her house. Incidentally, John also writes to a female church leader, as indicated in 2 John 1:1,5,13 if

---

9 The two are mentioned together seven times, five of which name Priscilla first, indicating she was equal to, if not more prominent than her husband.

understood straightforwardly.

Pray-ers and Prophets
1 Corinthians 11:2-16 urges women to pray and prophesy publicly, while maintaining propriety and gender distinctions in dress.

Equal Partners
Galatians 3:28 says 'There is neither Jew nor Greek, there is neither bond nor free, there is not male and female, for you are all one in Christ Jesus.' Concerned as it is with inheritance, this passage emphasizes that, just as under the Law, daughters could inherit as well as sons (Numbers 27:1-11; 36:1-13). We all, both men and women, inherit by being in Christ who inherits for us and we in him.

It is not surprising that the word for 'one' here – all 'one' in Christ Jesus – is masculine, for the masculine gender is always used for males and females collectively. This is no more an argument for masculine superiority or preference than the fact that we all being called a virgin in 2 Corinthians 11:2 implies that females are superior. As 'seed' is neuter in the Greek, and since we are Abraham's seed, to be neuter, according to this reasoning, would be preferred!

The passage asserts that Old Testament barriers of the law are irrelevant in Christ, that we may all participate freely by faith, women equally with men; race and social status are also irrelevant. The definition of 'male *and* female' as opposed to 'Jew *or* Greek' and 'bond *or* free' almost certainly is an allusion to Genesis 1:27. In that verse, humanity in its creation is seen as a unity before the distinction of gender is mentioned.

Overview of 1 Corinthians 11-14 and 1 Timothy 2-3

The problems apparent in both the Corinthian and Ephesian Churches were similar, and this is reflected in the many common themes and ideas in these letters. Both 1 Corinthians 11–14 and 1 Timothy 2–3 are concerned with church order, and Paul gives practical scriptural wisdom in dealing with situations in the churches. The passages substantiate one another, and we can enumerate thirteen ideas common to both, which are shown in the table overleaf.

1 Corinthians	Theme	1 Timothy
11:1-3	Mediatorship of Christ	2:5-6
11:3-16	Family relationships	2:8-13; 3:1-13
11:3-12	Exposition of Adam and Eve	2:13-15
11:4-16	Praying and prophesying	2:1,2,8,9
11:4-16	Clothing/hairstyles	2:8-9
11:10	Angels	3:16
11:16	Do not be contentious	3:3,11
11:17–14:33	Proper behaviour in church	2:7; 3
12:13-14	Body of Jews and Gentiles	2:7; 3:16
13	Faith, love, hope	2:15
14:28-40	Peacefulness among the women	2:2,1-12
14:34-40	Teaching/learning	2:7-12
14:34	Submission to church order	2:11-12

Conclusion

Despite his reputation as being anti-women Paul was probably the second greatest equalitarian in history, with Jesus being the first. Paul picked up where Jesus left off, treating women as equals, honouring them and giving them authority, breaking many social boundaries in the process.

We must now consider the traditional interpretations of 1 Corinthians 11–14 and 1 Timothy 2 in the light of our principles of interpretation and Paul's general attitude towards women.

7

Unfit Outfits

Is it proper for a woman to pray to God with her head uncovered?

1 Corinthians 11:13

I want women to adorn themselves with proper clothing, modestly and discretely, not with braided hair and gold or pearls or costly garments.

1 Timothy 2:9

Issue 1: Hair and Clothing

The first issue that arises is that of hair, head coverings, clothing and jewellery. When Paul writes 1 Corinthians, he urges women not to abandon their hair coverings, but in 1 Timothy, written over ten years later and in a different place and culture, he merely requires them to keep hairstyles modest and unshowy, which presupposes that their hair could be seen. This strongly suggests that the issue about hair and clothing was cultural.

If we understand that these passages teach essentially the same thing, albeit in a complementary way, then difficulties with some of the idiosyncratic material concerning loose or braided hair, obscure first-century head coverings and other cultural matters will be seen to be less important for interpretation than the main thrust of these passages, which concerns the status of women.

One of the persistent difficulties in interpreting these passages is the amount of speculative material which is introduced into the text in order to make it meaningful in every detail. The fact that Paul's writing in this section seems so obscure to us indicates he was referring to things which both parties understood but that we do not, probably specific cultural matters and previous letters. This means that many of the controversies rage around our guesswork as to what the historical and cultural connotations were, rather than what are the words of the Lord for us today and for all time.

We will first tackle 1 Corinthians 11 where Christian women appear to be enjoined to wear a veil or some sort of covering for the head, and then look briefly at 1 Timothy 2.

Historical Assumptions

Literal interpretation of these verses has resulted in churches in many traditions around the world adopting rules where women must wear veils or head scarves to cover their hair in church.

Other traditions maintain that husbands are the head of the household and have authority over their wives based upon this passage but dismiss the issue of headcoverings as cultural.

Structure

This passage is in the context of:

a   not letting our liberty of conscience cause any to stumble or invite judgement (1 Corinthians 10:29-30)

b   doing everything to the glory of God (1 Corinthians 10:31)

c   not giving offence to any cultural and ethnic distinctions which now meet together (1 Corinthians 10:32), but to act appropriately

d   imitate Paul as he imitates Christ (1 Corinthians 11:1).

Keywords

Cover

The same Greek root word for cover here, is used in the Septuagint for the word 'cover' in Leviticus 13:45 and the negative 'uncover' in Numbers 5:18. In these verses, the word 'covering' is used in connection with dressing, or loosing the hair, with or without a veil.

Men and women

In Greek, as in many languages, the words 'man' (*anēr*) and 'woman' (*gynē*) are also used to mean 'husband' and 'wife'. Therefore we need to rely on the context of the passages to determine whether Paul is referring to men and women in general, or specifically to husbands and wives. Paul quotes from Genesis 2 to support his assertions (1 Corinthians 11:7-9), which refers to a man and woman being one flesh, and lays the foundations for married men and women, teaching them how to relate together as partners. This indicates that Paul is talking about the relationship between husbands and wives, not about how all men relate to all women.

Head

As in English, the Greek word 'head' *(kephalē)* has a number of literal and metaphorical meanings, and can refer to a literal head – that on ones shoulders – or a metaphorical head either as in 'chief' or 'ruler', or as in 'source'.

In this passage the word 'head' switches between meaning a literal head and a metaphysical head. Some commentators have argued that when used metaphorically *kephalē* must be a hierarchical word, and as such a wife is ruled by her husband-head[1], however this has been adequately and comprehensively dismissed by Gordon Fee's analysis[2]. The metaphorical use of

---

1 For example Grudem, *Does "Head" Mean 'Source' or 'Authority over' in Greek Literature? A survey of 2,336 Examples*, Trinity Journal, 1985

2 Cf. G Fee, *1 Corinthians*, Eerdman, NICONT 1987, pages 498-512

kephalē to mean 'chief' is extremely rare, and in the vast majority of cases it means 'source', even when referring to Christ, who is the source of the Church. Head, as in 'source' is the meaning that the average Corinthian would have understood as they read Paul's letters, and not 'ruler'.

Authority

The Greek word *exousia* is sometimes translated as authority, or power, however its predominant use in the New Testament is to express liberty, or the power/right to choose. *Exousia* is never used passively to mean that someone has authority over someone else. Paul uses *exousia* here in 11:10, but he also uses it three times in chapter 9, where each time it is to be understood as 'right':

> v4 Do we not have a *right* to eat and drink?
> v5 Do we not have a *right* to take along a believing wife?
> v6 Or do only Barnabas and I not have a *right* to refrain
>   from working?

This should be remembered when we come to look at verse 10.

Angels

The meaning of 'because of the angels' in verse 10 is puzzling. Angels appear at the first mention of the house of God (Genesis 28:12,17,18), and appear in four places in 1 Corinthians – 4:9; 6:2-3; 11:10 and 13:1, as well as 1 Timothy 3:16. Maybe this was to remind the saints as they gathered that the unseen world was looking in and viewing their fitness and stance for the day when they will take on some of the angels' tasks (Hebrews 2:5).

Or maybe the newly emancipated charismatic women were saying that the resurrection was past and they were all like the angels now (cf. Luke 20:35-36; 1 Corinthians 15:12; 2 Timothy 2:17-18), thereby confusing or trying to lose the creatorial sex distinctions with men. Are the angels offended because the women have lost their distinctive dress or because they have not kept the proper order? (Jude 1:6)

Application

The first thing to note is that Paul expects women to be allowed to pray and prophesy publicly and not be restricted as they would have been under contemporary Judaism or Greek culture. While these verses address a problem arising out of a first-century cultural situation, it is clear that this passage is teaching something of fundamental relevance for all time, including the age in which we live. This is seen in the fact that it speaks of headship as found in the Godhead and reflected in the creatorial relationship of husband and wife. While the husband and wife relationship exists, these matters will always be relevant.

However, this passage is not primarily concerned with a piece of headgear, which is obvious given that Paul's instructions are founded on Genesis chapters 1 and 2, before clothing existed (Genesis 2:25). Paul is teaching on the husband-wife relationship, and the way that hair was worn or covered was the way this issue found expression in Paul's day. By comparison to 1 Timothy 2:8-9, we see this expression was subject to culture and circumstances.

1 Corinthians 11:6 says: '*If* it is a dishonour for a woman to be shorn or shaven ...' Presumably there could be conditions or cultures where it is not a dishonour. For instance, when a woman had finished her Nazarite vows, to shave her head would be an honour rather than a shame (Numbers 6:2-18). In a similar way, it would have been an honour, not a disgrace (1 Corinthians 11:14) for Paul to have worn his hair long in Corinth, as he did (see Acts 18:18). In our culture, many women wear their hair short (or not at all), and many men wear theirs longer, and neither is shamed.

So what is the question Paul is answering? Elsewhere in Corinthians, there are references to divisions between Christians from Jewish and Gentile backgrounds. The 'traditions' Paul refers to in verse 2 are neither Jewish nor Gentile as it seems that men kept their heads uncovered while the women covered theirs – these may represent a compromise between the merging cultures. The question appears to be that if women are allowed to pray and prophesy, like men should they uncover their heads or not?

As noted in chapter 6, Jewish wives attending the love feast (1 Corinthians 11:20) would wear a veil or head covering to indicate they were married. Greek men attending public feasts were never accompanied by their wives, instead taking along professional escorts, who would not cover their heads or dress their hair – loose hair would have had sexual connotations. It seems that either the Jewish practice of wives covering their heads in public worship was contested by those advocating more freedom, or the Greek practice of women not covering their heads was contested by some, who saw it as shameful, or possibly both (1 Corinthians 11:16).

Imagine the disgrace and offence that would have ensued as the Gentile women of the young Corinthian church, or Jewish women emancipated by their new faith in Christ, appeared in public worship looking like men, praying and prophesying with their heads uncovered. With their hair visible and even loose, the women would seem to be flaunting themselves in a sexual manner and thus appearing to reject their married status and their husbands.[3] For some, their appearance would approximate too closely to participants or priests in the mystery religions. How could Jew and Gentile have fellowship together at the Lord's table while such behaviour was giving offence?

Paul's general advice to avoid conflict and giving offence is 'Judge for yourselves' and don't be contentious (1 Corinthians 11:13). This is hardly a command of the Lord for all time (see 1 Corinthians 7:6,25), but a recommendation on the basis of how other churches under Paul's apostleship were handling this problem. Nonetheless, to quote Gordon Fee on this passage, 'for Paul, it does not seem to be a life and death matter.'[4]

If they are unable to judge and not be contentious, Paul then outlines three solutions to help aid them to reach a decision:

---

3 It would be like a married woman today taking off her wedding ring.

4 See Gordon D. Fee, *The First Epistle to the Corinthians*, NICONT, Eerdmans: Grand Rapids, 1987, page 530.

1) Authority and interdependence

Verse 10 states 'the woman (wife) ought to have authority on her head'. One historical interpretation of this is 'a symbol of authority on her head', indicating that covering the hair was a symbol of a husband's authority over his wife. However, as demonstrated on page 68, in 1 Corinthians 9 Paul uses the word *exousia* three times when talking about liberty or right to choose. So the text most likely reads 'the woman ought to have the right to choose on her head' - i.e. her status as a wife gives her rights, or that she can choose whether to wear a headcovering or not.

Paul is not dealing with who has authority (headship) over whom, but with the relationship between husband and wife. He argues (v3), that Christ is the source of every Christian man (cf. Colossians 1:18). Man is the source of woman, alluding to Genesis 2:22 (Paul does not say, as some translations do, that woman was made 'for the sake of man' but was made 'through' (*dia*) man)[5] and God is the source of Christ[6].

The Church metaphorically shows the glory of God, namely Christ, by men uncovering their heads, and wives who are the image and glory (likeness cf. Genesis 1:26-7, 5:1-2, 9:6) of God, are also the glory of man, covering their heads so that only God's glory is in the church and incidentally their glory, their hair, is not being displayed. Wives should acknowledge that their marriage status comes from, and reflects, the glory of God, not themselves.

Nothing is being said as to husbands ruling their wives, only that woman was sourced from man (Adam and Eve) and man sources from woman (i.e. all men and women). So, in the Lord neither is independent of the other (v11).

---

5 Note also in verse 12 Paul says that the woman is *ek* – 'out of' – the man, but even the man is *dia* 'through' the woman. It is worth noting that verse 8 should begin 'Now,' or 'Moreover,' rather than 'For,' indicating that this is the beginning of new idea.

6 Probably in Incarnation (John 1:14) – but it is not wrong to see the source as eternal and ontological also if we understand the Father's eternal generation of the Son.

2) Hair for a covering

If some women wish to regard their hair as a veil, this too is permissible. In verses 14-15, Paul points out that women naturally have longer hair and men naturally have shorter hair, and that a woman's hair is given to her as a covering, or veil[7].

3) No such doctrine

The correct translation of verse 16 is important to understand Paul's recommendations and revolves around the Greek word *toiautēn* which means 'such' or 'like'. Surprisingly, some translations, including both NIV and NASB, while rendering this word correctly 56 out of 57 times, here choose to translate it as 'other', which is the opposite meaning! This results in the verse reading 'we have no other practice', seemingly implying that everywhere else women do cover their heads. Paul's actual response is to appeal to cultural propriety, and to say that he and the churches of God had no custom of enforcing such proprieties with all the resulting pressure on etiquette between the sexes.

These three views each have meaning, but none is obligatory. It may be preferable for a recognised order in each church, but he is not saying that one practice should take precedence over another as long as propriety and marriage and gender distinctions are maintained. This is why Paul does not say 'thus says the Lord', and when dealing with the subject in Timothy says '*I* am not permitting'.

1 Timothy 2 8-9

In 1 Timothy 2:8-9, Paul suggests that women should not dress ostentatiously with braided hair, but modestly. The fact that in one passage Paul talks about hair being covered, and in the other talks about uncovered hair not being braided strongly indicates that both passages are contextual, but that there are important issues of church order which need to be addressed.

---

7 The word for 'veil' here is different from the word used in verse 6 for 'cover'

8

'Let the women keep silence'

> The women are to keep silent in the churches; for they are not permitted to speak
>
> 1 Corinthians 14:34

> A woman must quietly receive instruction with entire submissiveness
>
> 1 Timothy 2:11

Issue 2: Silence

The first passage in which Paul appears to place this restriction around women is 1 Corinthians 14:34-40. Here 'silence' is required of the wives.

Historical Assumptions

These verses have been used to restrict the role of women in church. Very few churches, if any, have applied them to mean total silence, but some have restricted women from preaching. To be consistent they ought to also have prevented women from singing, given that the same Greek word is used to describe both (see note on *Speak* on page 74).

Structure

This passage is in the context of:

a order in the church (1 Corinthians 11)

b order in the use of spiritual gifts (1 Corinthians 12)

c faith, hope and love (1 Corinthians 13)

d order in prophecy (1 Corinthians 14:1-33).

Keywords

Men and women

As described in the previous chapter, 'man' (*anēr*) and 'woman' (*gynē*) are also used to mean 'husband' and 'wife'. It appears from the references to Genesis 1–3 that Paul is referring to husbands and wives, as well as from verse 35 where wives are enjoined to learn from their own husbands at home.

Silence

In 1 Corinthians 14 the word 'silence' – *sigatō* – is used three times, in verses 28, 30 and 34. In verse 28 it is used to mean that the gift of tongues is to be limited, that is, silenced under certain conditions. Similarly, a prophet (verse 30) must be silent if some other revelation is being given. Furthermore, in 1 Timothy 2:11, the word for 'quietly' – *hesuchia* – is the same as that used in verse 2 of the same chapter, to refer to the type of life Christians can expect to enjoy under a benevolent secular government. It is normally translated 'peaceful' or 'quiet', certainly not 'silent'!

Speak

The word 'to speak' used in verse 34 – *laleo* – is a verb with a wide range of meaning in the area of speech. It literally originates from 'saying la la la' and has a lyrical quality. While it embraces many forms of verbal expression, it is used by Paul in Ephesians 5:19 for singing, and can be understood as 'chatter' or 'babble'.

Application

Complete silence?

There is no doubt that the silence Paul intends is not total. Under the grace of the New Covenant, if total silence were the rule women would have been more restricted than under the law (verse 34), a situation hardly likely to occur in the light of Jesus' attitude.

Praying and prophesying by women has already been accepted and encouraged in 1 Corinthians 11:5. Paul can hardly be made to contradict himself by the time he reaches chapter 14. Praying, prophesying, singing and presumably speaking in tongues and giving interpretation (1 Corinthians 14:14-15; Acts 1:14; 2:4) cannot be what 1 Corinthians 14:34-5 is concerned with. It might be questioned whether we are yet in the age of Pentecost if the women are never heard to do such things (Acts 2:17).

Qualified silence

It is discernible from the text that the 'silence' referred to is a qualified one (see verses 28,30). Women – or 'wives' – are to be silent (verse 34), but under what conditions? Verse 35 indicates what is in view: teaching is proceeding in the meeting and questions may be asked, but Paul calls for silence from the women so that they may learn. They are not to chatter among themselves, nor to question their husbands publicly, but to ask their own husbands at home, so as not to disturb the order of the meeting. Wives would often be at a great disadvantage compared to their husbands, since they were not educated, and their questions resulting from ignorance would hinder the flow of teaching in the meeting.

It must be remembered that the church at Corinth originated from the Jewish synagogue (Acts 18:7) then moved next door. The usual practice in the synagogue would be for the women (wives) to sit together chatting since they were not expected to learn. Most wives would be ignorant and unlearned, if not illiterate. Now that they have been liberated to learn in the church, many of their questions would appear trivial or irrelevant.

Jewish rabbis despised teaching women – 'Let the words of the law be burned rather than committed to women.' Such sentiments are hardly going to encourage a woman to study God's law, even if she were able to find anyone to help her. The result of this attitude in the synagogue and its effect in some of the majority Jewish churches, like the one at Corinth, would be inconsequential chatter among the women during the teaching.

In fact, this may be true not only for the first century but also the twenty-first: in many cultures the practice of religion is considered to be the prerogative of men, and women are discouraged from learning. To this day in some societies women are shown little if any respect, and there is still a need for these verses of exhortation. If, on the other hand, women were expected to understand and have an opinion, they would not need an injunction to quietness and good order, as was necessary in the synagogue and also apparently, at the church in Corinth.

Richard and Catherine Clark Kroeger[1], point out that the command in 1 Timothy 2:11 – 'A woman must quietly receive instruction with entire submissiveness' – was a well-known phrase used to describe the appropriate attitude of any disciple in the ancient Near East, and that for Paul to decree that women should assume an equal position with male students reveals an enlightened and liberating stance.

Set in order

In understanding Paul's injunction in this way, we see that the whole passage and its argument is about order in the meeting of the church. The use of gifts, the giving of tongues, the conduct of prophets and of the women is to be 'decent [beautiful] and in order' (verse 40).

---

1 *I Suffer Not a Woman,* Grand Rapids, Baker Book House, 1992.

Verses 34 and 35 say that it is neither decent nor beautiful for women to chatter and not learn. Instead, they are to be 'in order as also says the law'.

Thus says the law

'As also says the law' has been seen as a difficulty. As shown in chapter 2, nowhere in the Old Testament is there the slightest hint that silence is commanded for women. On the contrary, there is much evidence against it.

Some have tried to suggest that Paul is quoting the oral law found in the Talmud, which contained passages silencing women. If this is so, Paul has departed from his universal use of the word 'law' and has sided against Jesus[2]. Surely we cannot charge him with this!

However, these difficulties are overcome if we realise we are not to look in the Law of Moses nor even the rest of the Old Testament for commands prohibiting women from speaking. Rather, we should search for instruction concerning conduct in worship.

Large parts of the Old Testament laws and ordinances are concerned with correct order and conduct during worship, for example, much of Exodus, Leviticus, Numbers and Deuteronomy. There are also many cautionary tales of what happens when proper order and conduct in worship is abandoned. Notable examples include Korah's rebellion in Numbers 16, the 'strange fire' of Nadab and Abihu (Leviticus 10:1-2), the sin of Eli's sons and their resulting judgement (1 Samuel 2:12-17; 22-25), Uzza being struck down for his irreverence in grabbing the Ark (2 Samuel 6:6-7) and Uziah being struck with leprosy for his corruption of the temple (2 Chronicles 26:16-21).

Of course, Old Testament practice was very different from New, with its institutions and instructions concerning priests, Levites,

---

2 See Mark 7:1-13, where Jesus warns about the Pharisaism of making the word of God of no effect through vain tradition

sacrifices, incense, singing and so on. However, the principle of worshipping in the beauty of holy array or attire (Psalm 29:2; 110:3) is just as true for the new forms of the Christian age. In Colossians 2:5 Paul speaks of rejoicing as he beholds the Colossians' order (cf. also 1 Chronicles 25:5-6; Luke 1:8). Beautiful and orderly assemblies were enjoined in the old form of worship and are here encouraged in various ways in the new.

Conclusion

In conclusion it is clear that Paul advocated beauty and order in the worship of the early church, which involved using gifts, prophecy and speech in an orderly way.

1 Corinthians 14:34-40 does not say that women should be silent or that they are under obedience to men or even to their husbands[3]. Indeed it simply states that all are 'under order' when it comes to procedures of worship and assembly. This point is picked up again by Paul in 1 Timothy 2:11-12, which we look at in the next chapter.

---

3 Genesis 3:16 is a prophetic statement, not a command – cf. Genesis 4:7, for instance, where both words, 'desire' and 'rule' are used in relation to our attitude to sin.

9

Teaching and Usurping Authority

I do not permit a woman to teach or to have authority over a man

1 Timothy 2:12

Issue 3: Teaching and Leading

Such a statement from the apostle Paul appears to be clear, straightforward and incontrovertible as to its meaning. How then are we to understand it in relation to the rest of Scripture?

Traditional assumptions

The 'traditional' understanding of Paul's arguments here are that a woman may not teach and take authority over a man because:

a   **Adam was made before Eve** (1 Timothy 2:13). Therefore he has the authority. Surely this would suggest that, among other things, all older women should teach younger men on the basis of seniority.

b   **Adam was not deceived.** Adam is considered a better leader (verse 14) because he was not in deception. As discussed in chapter 1, this is hardly acceptable. If Adam fully knew that he was rebelling, then his sin was graver. If Eve did not know, she falls into the same category as Paul in 1 Timothy 1:13, that is, she receives mercy because she did it in ignorance. Besides this, the same passage of Scripture, Genesis 3, and the same Greek root for 'deceive' is used by Paul in 2 Corinthians 11:3 to warn the whole church, both men and women, not to be deceived.

c   **Women must not teach or lead ... their proper function is childbearing and they will be saved if they submit to that role in faith and love and holiness with modesty** (verse 15). So the argument runs! But what kind of salvation are we talking about? If women's eternal salvation rests on childbearing, what does the childless woman do? And, more importantly, what has happened to the atonement of Jesus Christ? If, alternatively as some say, it means that women will be kept safe through childbirth, then what can we say about godly women who have died while giving birth? Either way, this is a most unsatisfactory interpretation.

If we take verses 13-15 at face value, then women should not be entrusted with the teaching of children, who are certainly more vulnerable to possible heresy than men. And what of the wider world? The question must be asked how it is that a universal principle based on a 'creational ordinance' can be restricted only to circles of religious activity. If it is the will of God that women never teach men or operate in positions of authority over men, how can a theologian conclude that this need not apply to society as a whole? Surely the Church needs to speak out against the many contraventions of God's guidelines evident in the realms of business, education and even politics, where women are operating in senior leadership roles around the world.

So, whatever interpretation is placed upon this passage, this widely disseminated 'traditional' view of 1 Timothy 2:11-15 can never be acceptable. Some of the 'reasonings' attributed to Paul here have even been apologised for by commentators as they have admitted the weakness of what they think are Paul's arguments! How insulting to Paul to suggest that he needed to employ such flawed and feeble 'reasoning' to support his teaching - to say nothing of the Holy Spirit's inspiration! There must be a better interpretation of this passage.

Structure

The following analysis of 1 Timothy 2 was first pointed out to us by Wally Fahr, former elder of Cholmley Evangelical Church, and a Counsellor in north London. The chapter is in three paragraphs, introduced by three positive exhortations.

Verse 1: I *urge* that prayer be made continually;

Verse 8: I *want* both men and women to back up their prayers by godly lifestyles;

Verse 11: *Let women learn* quietly and without interrupting. The need for women to learn is in stark contrast to the culture of the time.

The repetition of 'quietness' in verses 11 and 12 suggests that the sentence coming between the two exhortations to quietness enjoined on women is a parenthesis to that admonition[1], however, there are no such things as brackets in original Greek[2]. Following the parenthesis, in verses 12-15 three reasons are now given from Genesis 2–3. Note that these are reasons why women *are to learn*, not reasons why women are to keep quiet.

These three reasons refer in order to the creation (verse 13), the deception (verse 14) and the fall and redemption (verse 15).

---

1 So that the verse looks like this: 'A woman must quietly receive instruction with entire submissiveness (but I do not allow a woman to teach or exercise authority over a man, but to remain quiet).'

2 Compare the same pattern in Romans 5:14,17 and Ephesians 3:1,14 when Paul clearly speaks parenthetically; some versions indicate this by brackets or dashes.

a   **Creation** (verse 13). Adam was formed first, *then* Eve. If
    Paul wanted to say that only men should teach on account
    of their priority in the creation order, he would have stated
    'Adam was formed first, *not* Eve'. In Christ, women as well
    as men must come into the fullness of maturity by learning
    and not remaining spiritual babies. As in the first creation,
    Eve's development followed Adam's, so it is in the new.[3]

b   **Deception** (verse 14). Eve was deceived, and so will her
    daughters be if they do not learn.

c   **Fall and redemption** (verse 15). Literally, '*she* shall be
    saved through the childbearing'. Eve was promised by
    God to be the childbearer of the Saviour (Genesis 3:15). Of
    course, it was through Mary that the promise was fulfilled
    and her example encourages other women to bring forth
    God's word to the world. Now *they*, that is, all of Eve's
    daughters, will be vindicated if they, like men also, continue
    in faith and love. (Note the change from 'she' to 'they' in the
    Greek text: '*she* will be saved ... if *they* continue'.)

Keywords

'I do not allow'

Paul is clearly giving his own advice for a specific situation, not
commands from God for the Church for all time.

Quietness

As shown on page 74, 'silence' does not mean total silence, as
indicated by the related adjective in 1 Timothy 2:2: 'a quiet ... life'.

Profess

The word *epangellomai,* translated 'profess' or 'professing' in 1
Timothy 2:9-10 is normally translated 'promise' elsewhere (see

---

3 Following the Genesis chapter 1 creation order of land, vegetation, fish, birds,
  animals and man, it is more logical to argue that woman represents the pinnacle
  of God's creative activity and, therefore, is superior to the rest of creation!

Romans 4:20-21; Titus 1:2; 2 Peter 2:19)[4]. It means 'offering promises', and, according to Professor Ramsey was used of political candidates seeking votes and of religious teachers offering a way of salvation or godliness[5].

Teaching

In the New Testament, the word 'teach' is not confined to describing a formal course of instruction. It may be used as in Matthew 28:15, where the elders merely asserted one statement (verse 13) 'and the soldiers were taught thereby'. This use of the word 'teach' is not uncommon (see Hebrews 8:11; 1 Corinthians 11:14; Luke 4:36; Mark 1:27; 1 Timothy 4:1; Revelation 2:14).

Take authority

The Greek word used here – *authentein* – often translated 'take authority', may contain overtones of self-assertion. The word is made up of two parts: 'self' and 'weapons'. Although it can be translated as 'taking authority' as recent work has demonstrated, nonetheless *exousia* would be more commonly used in that instance. It is significant that this is the only occurrence of the word anywhere in the entire Bible, and therefore would seem to be used to imply something different from the regular word for authority. 'Domineer' is a possible rendering.

Men and women

As described before, 'man' (*anēr*) and 'woman' (*gynē*) also mean 'husband' and 'wife'. From his use of Genesis 2–3, Paul is again referring to husbands and wives in this passage.

---

4 The NIV translates this word as 'promise' or 'a promise' 67 out of the 69 times it occurs. Twice they translate it as 'profess' or 'professed', both times in 1 Timothy. This surely should be considered a special pleading for this verse, which should be translated 'promise'

5 See Katherine Bushnell, *God's Word to Women,* point 332, available free online at www.godswordtowomen.org

Application

Good order

As in 1 Corinthians 14:34-40, during the teaching section of the public meeting, the women are exhorted not to chatter (which was common when women were not expected to learn), but to be quiet and orderly. Paul is not forbidding women to speak publicly.

Both passages are concerned with church order, and both are preceded by directions on suitable dress and behaviour for women while they are praying or prophesying publicly[6].

In 1 Timothy 2:9-10, Paul exhorts women who 'promise godliness', that is, those who proclaim the way of God to others, to dress and behave appropriately as they are prophesying and teaching. This needs to be borne in mind when reading Paul's remark two verses later in 1 Timothy 2:12.

The apparent contradiction is the same as that highlighted in 1 Corinthians 11:5 and 14:34. The same Paul can hardly be understood to be giving women directives concerning their behaviour and dress when speaking publicly, and then almost immediately forbid them to speak at all.

Adam and Eve

So what kind of teaching is Paul forbidding? In 1 Timothy 2:12-13 Paul shows what he has in mind by carefully and appropriately using Eve's behaviour in Genesis 2 and 3 as an example of what he is not permitting. Eve did not deliver a formal exegesis from a Bible passage, but out of her ignorance - for she was not with Adam when the command was given concerning the tree of knowledge – she asserted her viewpoint and so dictated to her husband. It is this sort of procedure within the teaching of the assembled church that Paul wisely forbids. As such, wives who up until that point were uneducated, were precluded from teaching out of their limited understanding. Rather they should learn.

---

6 Compare 1 Corinthians 11:1-16, and 1 Timothy 2:8-9

Taking authority versus submission

It is interesting to notice how little, in comparison with Christians today, the New Testament is concerned with the concept of church 'authority'. Authority is a rare feature of Early Church order. Even words translated 'rule' and 'obey' usually imply 'guidance' and 'hearkening to'. In the Middle East shepherds guide their flocks from in front rather than driving them from the rear – the sheep recognise their voice and follow them.

That such a unique New Testament and strong a word as *authentein* is introduced at this point hardly suggests that we are talking about a pastor's care over his or her flock, or in his or her teaching capacity. Philip Payne comments that:

> In no other verse of Scripture is it stated that women are not to be in authority over men. It is precarious indeed to deny that women should ever be in a position of authority over men based on the disputed meaning of the only occurrence of this word anywhere in the Bible.[7]

The use of a different word indicates a different kind of taking authority. Indeed, we are certainly not free to assume that it would be acceptable for a husband to '*authentein*' over his wife.

Aggressive assertions and opinions publicly delivered by a woman could be distasteful, out of order and embarrassing to her husband. A certain male sensitivity, despite centuries of chauvinism, is seen to have existed in ancient times, as in the story of Esther[8].

The exhortation for women to learn might appear to their husbands to be a threat to domestic tranquillity. So Paul quickly adds: 'By encouraging their spiritual education, I am not allowing women [wives] to teach and take authority [or, by taking authority] over men [husbands], but to learn "in quietness".' By this, he is

---

7 '*Libertarian Women at Ephesus*', Trinity Journal 1 (1980)

8 See Esther 1:16-20

saying nothing about the suitability of a Spirit-led woman teaching under the order of the church.

A woman could not be considered to be domineering by being a properly recognised teacher with authority to teach given by God and the church. But this passage is not concerned with this. Paul is concerned for the education of women in God's house after centuries of having been kept in ignorance, and how this should be conducted in a godly fashion. He simply gives his wisdom for the current situation – 'I permit not' (v12), in a similar way to 1 Corinthians 14.

While it is true that Paul describes the husband as 'head' of the wife, he describes the nature of that authority in Ephesians 5:21-33. It is not a domineering, authoritative role, but rather one of service and self-sacrifice in order to bring the wife to her full potential, as Christ does the Church. A similar thought must have been in Paul's mind when he says 'let the women learn' in 1 Timothy 2.

Moreover, in Ephesians 5:22-24, the exhortation to wives is to receive this kind of headship, or sourcing, from their husbands, just as the wives in 1 Timothy 2 are exhorted to receive the instruction of the church with all submission and respect.

Conclusion

In summary, we should understand both 1 Corinthians 11–14 and 1 Timothy 2 in this way. They are encouragements for women to participate publicly, providing that Paul's advice is borne in mind:

a   Women should dress appropriately and modestly;

b   Wives should honour their marriage relationship and the sourcing headship of their husbands;

c   Women should take the opportunity to learn and receive from others in a quiet and submissive spirit.

If 1 Timothy (and similarly 1 Corinthians) is a transcultural, timeless manual for all churches everywhere, then how are we to decide which of the points Paul makes are based on universal principles and which are not? For example, does 1 Timothy 5:20 come into this category? If so, why don't churches take this seriously today and include regular sessions of public rebuke? Similarly, should today's young widows marry and have children as a matter of theological principle (1 Timothy 5:14)? Here Paul uses exactly the same word for to will/wish – *boulomai* – as he does in the negative in 1 Timothy 2:12. Or what about Galatians 5:12, where Paul calls for troublemakers to castrate themselves? Or are these and other verses like them to be explained as situational?

Finally, it is worth emphasising that 1 Timothy was written around 63-5AD, after Paul and Timothy had been working together for fifteen years. Why would Paul need to tell Timothy not to let women teach? Would Timothy not have been aware of Paul's views on this?

If, however, some pressure came into the church to downgrade womanhood, and to neglect the teaching of women despite their emancipation through the gospel, then this injunction makes sense. Timothy must not give in to cultural traditions by neglecting the wives in the church. The subsequent history of the Church shows how important this injunction has been.

10

The Testimony of Church History

In 363AD, 330 years after the crucifixion, the Council of Laodicea disbanded the office of woman presbyter. Evidently this means that prior to this, women had a leading place in the function of the Church. Women deacons or ministers - the same masculine word in Greek is used for both men and women - were known in the New Testament. In 112AD Pliny wrote to the Roman Emperor Trajan about Christians. He wanted advice on how to deal with them and told Trajan that in order to find out more about their teachings he had tortured 'two female slaves who are called deacons.'[1]

The relegation of women in the territorial Constantinian church led many women with godly gifts to become independent 'mystics' or be involved in radical groups who attempted to bring renewal by re-emphasizing women's place in church ministry. These radical movements were, in turn, often violently crushed by the established church, who labelled them as 'heretics'.

Throughout Church history revival and renewal has followed the involvement of women in church leadership, ministry and support. Here we have listed a few examples from each century.

---

1 NB they were not called 'deaconesses'

1st Theodoret said that Phoebe was famous 'throughout the world. She was known not only to the Greeks and Romans but also the barbarians.' Even Tertullian said 'the holy Prisca (Priscilla) preached the gospel.' Eusebius wrote of Philip's daughters and John the Apostle as 'great lights which had gone out in Asia.'

2nd The brutal execution of Blandina in Lyon was recognised by the church as imitating Christ's death on the cross. Tied to the stake, she ministered forgiveness by the Spirit's flow (John 20:22-23). The Montanists also had renowned women prophets.

3rd Perpetua and Felicitas, mistress and slave girl, were notable among the growing number of martyrs – martyrdom was becoming a ministry. The mainstream church had different classes of women who served; widows, 'virgins', deacons and prophets.

4th The Priscillians of Spain learned the Scriptures through both male and female lay people. Euchrotia the widow of a poet was executed alongside bishop Priscillian for leading in this reform movement. By her learning and piety Macrina influenced her famous Cappadocian brother Basil to enter the ministry.

5th To avoid the worldly corruption that had invaded the church, the monastic movement retreated into the desert, attracting a large number of women. In this century there were an estimated 20,000 female ascetics, compared with only 10,000 males.

6th Brigit of Kildare formed her own community, led and taught men and women, evangelised and was prayed over by visiting bishop, Mel. When asked why he prayed the consecration prayer for a bishop over a woman, he replied, 'No power have I in this matter. That dignity has been given by God to Brigit.' Future abbesses of Kildare also had this episcopal honour.

7th Aidan the Scottish evangelist, set up mixed monasteries in England. Chief among the female leaders was Hilda, Abbess of Whitby, who trained many renowned male and female workers and bishops, including an archbishop.

8th Boniface was one of the last outstanding missionaries to leave the British Isles for nearly 1000 years. He was joined by Liboa, a female co-worker and counterpart, an abbess who taught on the Scriptures and Early Church Fathers. Like Brigit and Hilda before her, many miracles were attributed to her.

9th Women's ministry was becoming more restricted, and stories of a legendary nature are attributed to 'mystic' females. Nonetheless, when myth is discounted, godly women leaders such as Luitberga and Theoda emerge.

10th The institutional church instituted the Clunic Reform, establishing male dominance. The Nicolaitan 'heresy' reacted against the enforcement of celibatic priesthood, and many Celtic priests among others protested that they needed their wives to keep their bodies and souls together. This was an unusual but accepted female ministry to Christ!

11th The darkest century for women disciples coincided with the height of power of the institutional church. However in 1098, Hildergard von Bingen, the bright light of the next century, was born. From age eight she was spiritually tutored by Jutta of Spanheim, a mystic attached to a Benedictine abbey. Hildergard preached in the Rheinland, saw miracles, was sought after for her wisdom, effected reform and spoke in tongues. She humbly called herself 'a feather on the breath of God' and gained authority for her ministry from the Pope.

12th Despite being an offense punishable by death by the authorities, one in three Europeans were estimated to have attended a Waldensian conventicle. The Waldensians were nonconformist but orthodox Christians whose women preached, baptised, gave communion and were equal to their menfolk. Also, Christina was an Anglosaxon mystic who taught and discipled men and women.

13th This century saw the rise of 'the first women's movement' – the Beguines – a religious order of women that spread across Europe, who lived simple lives of service. They and their male counterparts, the Beghards, were often accused of heresy and persecuted to death by the Papal authorities.

14th Catherine of Siena was a reformer whose ministry was recognised and eventually canonised. Julian of Norwich lived in a cell in the wall of St Julian's church, allegedly to age 100. She wrote *Revelations of Divine Love,* and had extensive learning. She preached and counselled all who came to her.

15th Margery Kempe was a wandering evangelist who spent twenty years travelling from Palestine to Norway. A wife and mother of fourteen children, she began having visions and pursued holiness.

16th Among both Anabaptists and Polish Brethren, women ministered and taught, and were martyred alongside men. Katherine Zell was a great reformer and pleaded for tolerance for Schwenckfeld, Servetus and others murdered during the reformation. She and her husband were a model for the husband and wife ministry partnership.

17th The Quakers, from their outset established no distinctions between what men and women could do in ministry. George Fox, their leader, challenged those who limited women's ministry. Quaker women, including Elizabeth Hooton, Mary Fisher and Margaret Fell suffered much for their outspoken preaching.

18th John Wesley was the 'most ardent feminist of the eighteenth century'. When he heard people were opposing a woman preacher, despite her obvious gifting, he wrote: 'We give the right hand of fellowship to Sarah Mallett, and have no objection to her being a preacher in our connection, so long as she preaches Methodist doctrine and attends to our

discipline.' The Wesleys' mother, Susannah had a whole school of
theology – Practical Theology – attributed to her. The Moravians
in the eighteenth century had female elders.

19th A whole host of women preachers and missionaries
rose up, including the theologian of the Salvation Army,
Catherine Booth. William Booth, her husband, said 'my best men
are women.' The Salvation Army were the first Christian movement
to write in their official constitution that 'nothing shall authorize
the conference to take any course whereby the right of females to
be employed as evangelists or class leaders shall be impeded or
destroyed, or which shall render females ineligible for any office ...'
Space does not permit to tell of the army of heroic women who heard
God's call to overseas missions, particularly in the second half of the
nineteenth century, taking the gospel to the four corners of the world,
often in the most pioneering of situations. By 1904 there were 44
missionary societies staffed and run entirely by women.

20th It is surprising after a century festooned with great
Christian women that this issue still needed to be
addressed. A few names will have to represent a whole river
of devotion and obedience to our Lord. Dora Yu in China, the
evangelist who led Watchman Nee and his mother to Christ,
Kathryn Kuhlman in the USA, whose ministry in preaching and
healing was so manifestly owned by God and Jackie Pullinger-To
in Hong Kong, whose work among the poor and drug-addicted
has been so anointed and fruitful. Add to these the multiplicity
of women who have served in their home countries and overseas.
Not to mention the many women from the West Indies, Africa
and Asia who have preached the gospel, planted churches and
served the poor. Their names are written in heaven.

21st So where do we go from here? There are serious issues
to grapple with today as we seek to disciple women to
Christ and train anointed ones for Christian leadership.

11

Gender Issues Today

Where are we at in the UK today, and how did we get here?

In the Christian world today, we see many examples of effective female leadership throughout the denominations.

In many cultures of the world over the past century or two the rapid spread of Christianity with its message of liberation and empowerment of women, has affected the roles of women in the churches planted. The influence of women missionaries who were often the most impressive models for the new national Christians, left a life-long impact on many African and Asian Christian leaders. Because of them, gifted women are respected in those cultures and their giftings are usually welcomed in the church.

Wars in the West

In the West we have had a more varied history, as this book has attempted to describe. In Europe, the social and political history of the past 90 years since the First World War has seen dramatic shifts in the perception of women and their roles, both in society and in the church.

Virginia Nicholson in her book *Singled Out* gives an impressively researched overview of the changing roles and perceptions of women in the UK since the end of the 1914-1918 War. Prior to that time, it was expected that the vast majority of women would marry and have children. Those that didn't were often in domestic service anyway, so the defining role of women was still a domestic one. Women rarely worked outside the home once they were married. The Great War in Europe put an end to that era. For a start, many women were called on to serve their country during the War, by taking on jobs in factories, offices and farming, which had been left vacant by the millions of men called up to enlist as soldiers.

When the War ended, many women found it difficult to give up the freedom and empowerment that their working lives had provided. Even more significantly there were two million women who had lost their boyfriends, fiancés and husbands in the trenches of World War One and were now left with no men to marry. There was a huge imbalance in the ratio of men to women, made even worse by the numbers of men who returned from the War physically and mentally shot to pieces. Women had to find a way to survive on their own, and the great majority did. They carved out for themselves roles in society which were not dependent solely on the grace and financial favours of men. They were greatly helped in this by the feminist cause, which emphasised the dignity and worth of women, especially of single women who were given a very raw deal in society.

The Feminist Movement

Looking back on the past 50-100 years we can see the huge shift in attitudes to women and gender politics which has taken place in Western societies. One hundred years ago, women were mostly owned by men, either their husbands, their masters, if they were servants, or by their fathers, if they were single daughters. Of course, many men saw their protective roles as a sacred trust, but some took the opportunity to demean or exploit the women they owned. The feminist movement, which was gaining ground in the nineteenth century, challenged this vociferously, but its exponents were mostly concerned about protecting women from exploitation and abuse in their domestic and social lives rather than changing the perceptions of femininity. Christian women were frequently at the forefront of the campaigns for legal protection for women, campaigning for rights for wives, who could be 'dumped' penniless by husbands divorcing them, with the women having no rights over their children or even their own property.

Feminism continued to hugely impact Britain in the first half of the twentieth century, gaining ground in areas such as 'equal pay for equal work' and 'pensions for single women'. But after the Second World War, which once again, out of necessity, opened doors wide for women in the workplace, there began to be a shift. In order to stabilize society after two major wars in 30 years, there was a renewed emphasis in newspapers, magazines and advertising on the domestic role of women. The familiar images of the 1950's housewife, quaintly seen on old newsreels and in magazines of the era, emphasize her contentment with her domestic role, serving her husband and children. There was a strong message to women that the man was the head of the house, and her fulfilment would come as she submitted to him and sublimated her life and desires into his.

Socio-Biology

Behind this propagated image of cosy domesticity, which in itself was innocent and good, and very attractive to many women, lay the theory of biological determinism, that is, that women's and men's roles in life and society are determined and dictated by their gender. This not only decreed subservient roles for women as a matter of course, but also seemed to allow men the freedom to display the worst aspects of masculinity with impunity. Richard Dawkins' book *The Selfish Gene*, published in 1976, reverted to the pre-1950 biological determinism theme, and even seemed to some to give a let-out for male sexual sins such as adultery or rape (it's all in the genes!). This hardly helped the (often Christian) feminists who were campaigning for tougher sentences in the courts for crimes of rape and incest, for example.

Radical Feminism

In the 1960s, the old Liberal Feminism, which had done so much to alleviate injustice and oppression of women in society, began to be overtaken and superseded by Radical Feminism. Radical feminists aimed not just for equality with men, but at creating a woman-centred world to replace the man-centred one (they have had some success at this, as society has become more feminized, for good or ill). Biological functions such as pregnancy and motherhood were seen as restricting women, and were challenged on every hand. The Pill, abortion on demand, and 24-hour nursery care, were rallying cries to 'free' women from their biological destiny and limitations. Consciousness-raising groups were also instigated, to help to dispel the 'weaker vessel' concept. Self-defence techniques against sexual attacks, and self-assertion seminars, were ways in which feminism aimed to empower women to engage in the world on an equal footing with men. Many went further, seeing the need to 'feminize' men, by calling them to engage in roles previously seen as the responsibility of women. The 'New Man' emerged in the 1970s. He could cook, change a nappy, use a vacuum cleaner and empathize with his wife, who may have taken on the role of being the primary bread-winner for the household. Today, such adaptability on the part of men is common-place and commendable, but in the 1960s and 70s, it was quite a social revolution.

The emphasis on the 'sameness' rather than the 'difference' between the sexes, led to the feminist theory that masculine and feminine are social constructs rather than biologically caused. The different roles of men and women and their apparent strengths and weaknesses, were seen as the effects of social conditioning, rather than 'naturally' determined. There is obviously demonstrable truth in this, but it is not the whole story, as we argue in the next chapter.[1]

Post-Modernity

All this intellectual debate of the 1980s was somewhat overturned by the Post-Modern philosophies of the 1990s and beyond. All 'absolutes' and any single, unifying 'world view', whether based on biology or on socio-political power structures, were rejected by the new Post-Modernists. The fight of radical feminists against male domination was seen as irrelevant – a sign of capitulation to the meta-narrative of men's superiority, in seeking equality with them.

Post-modernism, with its emphasis on the rejection of absolutes, emphasised the fluidity of relationships and roles, the plurality of culture and the relativity of meaning. Women and men were encouraged to find out who they were by starting from within, subjectively and individually. Both the old patriarchal views and new liberal or gay lifestyles were accepted as individual choices. Gender concepts became more fluid as just ideas in the mind. Post-modernism encouraged everyone to 'do what was right for them', and find their own way through the gender questions. A huge amount of gender confusion resulted, as people tried to examine their psychologies, rather than their bodies, to determine their sex.

Perhaps in the light of this, and as a reaction to it, non-intellectual, gender psychology books also began to flood the market (*Why Men Don't Iron* and *Men are from Mars Women are from Venus*, etc.). Such books re-emphasised 'difference' according to 'nature' between the sexes, but did not attach value

---

1 For a fuller treatment of this subject see *What's Right with Feminism* by Elaine Storkey, SPCK, 1985

judgements or roles to gender differences as their pre-modern
counterparts did. The message was 'men and women act and
react differently, but that's ok!' Meanwhile in the new millennium
we have seen a pre-feminist return to the emphasis on woman's
sexual allure determining her value.

Female Sexualisation

Because radical feminists were concerned ultimately to 'liberate'
women in sexuality as well as society, they began to encourage
women to be 'empowered' by using their sex appeal as a means of
deliberately dominating men. 'Sex and the City' was born.

Whereas feminists of the 70s and 80s were campaigning
against beauty contests as demeaning to women, now it seems
that without sexual allure, women have 'failed'. Young girls are
sexualised at an earlier age than ever before and become obsessed
with their bodies and with the need to be sexually desirable as
well as successful in a male-dominated world. Natasha Water, in
her book *Living Dolls* paints a frightening picture of the hyper-
feminized, hyper-sexualized, hyper-pink culture which today
girls are being raised in. Despite the efforts of traditional feminist
groups to stem this tide a little (and to mount 'Pink Stinks'
campaigns!), most young girls are being brainwashed with
aspirations, not of intellectual achievements that could change
the world or help the poor, but of achieving a 'Barbie doll' figure
with long blonde hair and enhanced breasts, and maybe a career
in glamour-modelling or even as a call-girl. How on earth should
we respond as Christians to all this? Surely we have a calling to
show the world a more excellent way, to help girls discover their
true value and boys to develop their masculine strengths, without
the world's shallow agendas.

12

Masculinity and Femininity

Masculine and Feminine

It seems to us that if God made us 'male and female', then we will expect to see some differences, not only in our physical bodies, but in our psychologies that dwell in them. The apostle Paul says that 'in Christ Jesus there is no *male and female*' (Galatians 3:28). What does the phrase 'in Christ' mean? If we think of Paul's words in 2 Corinthians 5:17, 'If anyone is in Christ, he is a new creation', we can see that Paul is speaking of our spiritual life, not our fleshly one. In our spirits we have been regenerated and there is no gender distinction in that life. Before the throne of God we will worship him as those redeemed from every tribe and nation, but with nothing said about gender differences (Revelation 7:9).

However, in the flesh, there are differences. We think of it in this way: spiritually there is no difference between males and females, as we worship God and experience his life. In our bodies there are obvious differences, and no amount of unisex clothes and hairstyles will change that (though gender reconstruction surgery might do so, at least in part). But what about our psychology (our

soul, or our brain) where we think and feel and perceive ourselves
and the world? This will surely be shaped both by our physical
bodies and their hormonal effects, and by our regenerate spirits
that, in union with God, begin to receive 'the mind of Christ'.

Since we are created male and female in our bodies, we might
expect that the male and female hormones will have at least some
effect on our psyche. Women will probably tend toward feminine
behaviour and men toward masculine. This could mean that there
may be differences between men and women in their leadership
styles. In the charts on pages 102-103, which we devised many years
ago from a mixture of knowledge and observation, we have tried
to set out the different physical effects in the body, of masculine
and feminine hormones as well as genes, and have argued that
these physical effects are often played out in our psychologies as
well. Our aim as Christians should be to reflect the strengths of
both masculine and feminine (since both are found in Father God,
and seen in Jesus). We should also note the possible weaknesses
of our gender, and seek God's help to transform them!

Looking at these charts you may feel we are going back to
biological determinism but that is not so. It is true that male and
female hormones will affect our psychologies immensely, but as
individuals we all have a combination of male and female hormones
in our bodies in varying ratios, and we are by no means all clearly
stamped 'male' or 'female' in our psychology, even if we are in our
bodies. There is a continuum of expression from female to male
psychology and we are all at different places on it.

Let's Be Different!

In his book *The Essential Difference* Simon Baron-Cohen,
Professor of Psychology at Cambridge University, argues in a
similar way about gender differences. He calls it the male and
female brain, rather than psychology, but his underlying thesis is
much the same. Baron-Cohen argues that there are differences in

male and female brains, which have effects on behaviour, interests, skills and viewpoints. Making it clear that male and female brains do not necessarily correlate with male and female genders, he describes the male brain as 'Systemising', and the female brain as 'Empathic'. He also makes the point that some people have an extreme female or extreme male brain (he puts some autistic disorders in the latter category), and that some people have a 'balanced brain', which draws on both gender strengths.

The point he is making is that most males tend to have more of a male brain, and most females tend toward a female brain, but we cannot stereotype people. Hardly rocket science perhaps, but Baron-Cohen states in his preface that he felt he could not publish the fruits of his research twenty years earlier because feminist teaching of the time would not allow that there were differences, for fear of stereotyping and discrimination against women raising its ugly head again. Baron-Cohen is very clear, however, that he does not believe in stereotyping or discrimination! He simply believes there is a difference in the way we might expect boys and girls to develop.

Conclusion

In thinking about women functioning in leadership positions, we can see that they may need to draw on both sides of their brain in order to be as effective in the management and pastoral roles as they might wish. Many women leaders bring warmth, accessibility and pastoral sensitivity to their leadership role and tend to be 'team' players. If they also have the masculine strengths of vision, initiative, discipline and drive, then they make outstanding leaders, provided they can deal with the negative side of their strengths. Similarly, men who have added to their 'masculine' strengths the 'feminine' qualities of compassion, sensitivity and relational accessibility, become admirable leaders. The more 'balanced' we become, the more we overcome the weaknesses of our masculinity and femininity, the more we will fulfil the creation mandate to exercise leadership as male and female together.

Possible Differences in Male and Female Psychologies based on male and female genes activated by masculine and feminine hormones (see above)

a) Masculine Characteristics

Physical Effect of Sex and Hormones	Possible Psychological effects	
	Positive	Negative
Strong drive	Initiates, pushes through problems	Rides roughshod
Muscle power	Strength, active & protective	Aggression
Leanness	Disciplined, structured	Hard, unbending
Tough skin	Takes knocks	Insensitive
Broad Shoulders	Carries burdens well	Intimidating, dominating
Reproductive system outside the body	Non-complex relationships	Relationally shallow
Taller	Sees further	Impatient of detail, ignores needs close to
Emotionally and verbally restrained	Less vulnerable	Less ability to make and hold relationships

b) Feminine Characteristics

Physical Effect of Sex and Hormones	Possible Psychological effects	
	Positive	Negative
Passivity	Co-operative, submissive	Easily manipulated or controlled
Fat deposits	Gentle, comforting	Unboundaried, indulgent
Womb	Creative, nurturing	Possessive
Thin skin	Sensitive	Easily bruised and hurt
Skeletal structure	Carries burdens inwardly	Introspective, brooding
Reproductive system inside the body	Relates more intensely and deeply	Can get tangled and hurt in relationships
Shorter	Sees details and small needs	Disinterested in wider vision
Emotionally expressive	Verbally adroit, able to share and relate	Vulnerable to emotional hurt and depression

Afterword

In writing this book we have poured out the fruits of our study, prayer, meditation and experience over many years of serving the Church worldwide, as well as leading the Ichthus movement. From Genesis to Revelation, looking at the Old Testament, New Testament, Jesus and Paul, we have presented a consistent biblical case for releasing women's spiritual gifts and leadership potential. We have shown how women have been empowered and used by God in Church history, and have shared some of our insights into masculine and feminine psychology.

Some Christians express concern that different interpretations of Scripture will potentially result in more church division. It may or may not be an essential part of the gospel for you to believe in the equality of women and men (belief in the equality of racial groups and social status have also been disputed over the centuries). We have always taken the view that if you are confident before the Lord in your convictions and understanding, you can afford to be generous and gracious toward the viewpoints of others.

We believe in the unity of the Body of Christ, and have always worked to promote harmonious relationships between the denominations and streams. Our own convictions and practice have not prevented our fellowship with true believers in Jesus everywhere, whatever their persuasion.

We ourselves have worked for forty-five years as a husband and wife partnership in leadership and ministry. Our giftings are not identical nor totally interchangeable, but we both have known the clear calling of the Lord on our lives. If, in the age to come, we are going to be 'one' in Christ, then why not lay hold of the grace of God to practice our future now?